THE TEENAGE WEALTHYPRENEUR

7 SIMPLE STRATEGIES ON HOW TEENS CAN LEARN
MONEY MANAGEMENT AND WEALTH GENERATION

E.T. MULLONEY

© Copyright 2023 - **All rights reserved.**

The content contained within this book may not be reproduced, duplicated or transmitted without direct written permission from the author or the publisher.

Under no circumstances will any blame or legal responsibility be held against the publisher, or author, for any damages, reparation, or monetary loss due to the information contained within this book, either directly or indirectly.

Legal Notice:

This book is copyright protected. It is only for personal use. You cannot amend, distribute, sell, use, quote or paraphrase any part, or the content within this book, without the consent of the author or publisher.

Disclaimer Notice:

Please note the information contained within this document is for educational and entertainment purposes only. All effort has been executed to present accurate, up to date, reliable, complete information. No warranties of any kind are declared or implied. Readers acknowledge that the author is not engaged in the rendering of legal, financial, medical or professional advice. The content within this book has been derived from various sources. Please consult a licensed professional before attempting any techniques outlined in this book.

By reading this document, the reader agrees that under no circumstances is the author responsible for any losses, direct or indirect, that are incurred as a result of the use of the information contained within this document, including, but not limited to, errors, omissions, or inaccuracies.

TABLE OF CONTENTS

Introduction 5

1. UNDERSTANDING FINANCIAL CONCEPTS AND PRINCIPLES 9
   Why Financial Literacy Matters 10
   Basic Financial Concepts and Terminology 15
   Setting Financial Goals 19
   In Real Life 24

2. STRATEGY 1—CREATING A BUDGET AND MANAGING EXPENSES 27
   Understanding Your Income and Expenses 29
   Creating a Budget 31
   Tips for Reducing Expenses 34
   Sticking To Your Budget 39
   Do It Yourself 43

3. STRATEGY 2—SAVING AND INVESTING FOR THE FUTURE 47
   The Benefits of Saving Early 48
   The "Pay Yourself First" Principle 52
   Types of Savings Accounts and Investments 55
   Tips and Tricks to Invest Wisely 65
   In Real Life 67

4. STRATEGY 3—EXPLORING ENTREPRENEURSHIP 71
   What Exactly Is Entrepreneurship? 72
   What Does a Successful Entrepreneur Look Like? 75

Finding Your Passion ... 80
Starting Your Own Business ... 84
In Real Life ... 88

5. **STRATEGY 4—BUILDING WEALTH THROUGH REAL ESTATE INVESTING** ... 91
   Real Estate Investing and the Benefits ... 92
   The Different Types ... 95
   A Few Tips and Tricks ... 98

6. **STRATEGY 5—DEVELOPING A POSITIVE MONEY MINDSET** ... 103
   The Importance of the Money Mindset ... 104
   Don't Let Your Money Beliefs Limit You ... 107
   Creating a Positive Mindset About Money ... 110
   Take It Step By Step ... 115

7. **STRATEGY 6—NAVIGATING FINANCIAL CHALLENGES AND PITFALLS** ... 117
   Teenage Financial Challenges ... 118
   Credit and Debt ... 125
   Avoid the Pitfalls ... 128
   Whoops, I Messed Up! Now What? ... 132
   In Real Life ... 134

8. **STRATEGY 7—DEVELOPING EFFECTIVE MONEY HABITS FOR LONG-TERM SUCCESS** ... 137
   Developing Habits That Stick ... 139
   Getting Help and Support ... 144

   Conclusion ... 149
   References ... 153

INTRODUCTION

When I was 10, summer meant pure joy and endless exploration for me. Living on an island with my single mother, I cherished the simple pleasures of life—playing with cousins and immersing myself in nature's wonders. But, out of the blue, the weight of adulthood settled upon my shoulders. I was confronted with the challenge of navigating my finances and creating wealth, all without any guidance. There was no manual to follow, and school didn't equip me with the necessary knowledge. I had to figure it all out on my own, step by step.

I don't want to give the impression that my childhood was a breeze. Coming from a single-parent household meant we didn't have unlimited resources. I couldn't rely on my mom to fulfill all my material desires. The success I enjoy today is the result of my own hard work and determination. I take great pride in the journey that brought me here. Resilience, perseverance, and a strong sense of purpose were key elements of my story, teaching me valuable lessons along the way. You might be facing similar circumstances or come from a slightly more privileged background.

Regardless, as a teenager, we often neglect to consider our future and our financial well-being. It's easy to push these matters aside, thinking they only concern adults. But the truth is, our beliefs about money and finances are often shaped at a young age.

Starting early can be the key to success. You have a unique advantage—learning from the mistakes of others. By avoiding major financial mistakes and making smart investments, you can build wealth and thrive. Leave behind the struggles that others faced. Consider it a cheat code for becoming a financially savvy teen and achieving success.

My purpose is simple: to share the practical wisdom I've learned and help teenagers like you navigate the challenges of life. In this book, you'll discover valuable advice and insights to guide you toward financial independence. It's not just about knowing how to handle money; it's about developing a positive mindset and discipline toward handling your finances.

Discovering the key to something extraordinary—a task so simple that even a child can accomplish it. Prepare to unlock its hidden power and witness the remarkable impact it can have on your life. Are you ready to embrace this empowering secret? Don't let the complexity of numbers and terms overwhelm you; it's simpler than you think. Together, let's embark on this journey of discovery and unlock the keys to a brighter, more secure future. Get ready to witness the incredible results that await you.

In this book, we are going to be talking about seven strategies that can help you empower your financial future. We will be covering everything from creating a plan to budgeting and all the way to investing. These are things that you can start implementing right now so you can build up the habits that will take you into your future. Rest assured, your future self will be immensely grateful that you devoted this time to learn and develop. It will be a gift that keeps on giving throughout your adult life.

As we enter Chapter 1, we'll begin exploring essential financial concepts and principles. This lays the groundwork for the rest of the book, making everything easier to understand. From there, we'll delve into practical strategies to enhance your financial literacy. So, without further ado, let's dive right in!

1

UNDERSTANDING FINANCIAL CONCEPTS AND PRINCIPLES

"I am one who believes that all 10-year olds should have the competencies in reading and writing, and computation, which give them the potential to be lifetime learners. And I see financial education as an important part of that foundation of learning that children need to have in a world that is ever more complicated and requires that all of us understand computation and finance, and the implication of savings, because they are key to participating fully in what life has to offer in the United States."

— PAUL H. O'NEILL, U.S. TREASURY SECRETARY

WHY FINANCIAL LITERACY MATTERS

Financial literacy is one of the most important skills any teenager and young adult could have. When you are financially literate, it means that you understand finances and how to use it. If your dad were to give you a toolbox with all the tools you could ever need and told you to build a house would you be able to? Probably not. Even though you have everything you need, you don't know how to use it. The same thing applies to finances. Just because you have money doesn't mean you know how to use it properly. Understanding how money works and how to use it will help you to make better financial choices so you can build up your future. There are so many benefits to mastering finances that it is simply a must for every young person.

You Will Start to Understand the Value of Money

We all know that money has value. However, you can't fully comprehend the value of money unless you are managing it on your own and earning it for yourself. I'm sure you have heard your parents say something along the lines of, "Do you think money grows on trees?" At least, that's what my mother used to say to me. This was usually the staple response when I asked for something. At that time, I didn't understand the value of money. My single mother understood the value of money because she was working and earning it.

As you get older, you will need to understand how money works and how to manage it for yourself. Many young people tend to spend too much money on unnecessary items because they don't fully comprehend how to manage it properly. Earning your own money through doing small chores and jobs can really help you to see what it takes to earn money. When you are earning your own money through hard work, it puts more value on that money. You know that it doesn't just materialize in your wallet; you need to earn it. This is a valuable lesson because it helps you to plan and spend your money more wisely.

You Know What Is Really Important

There is a big difference between what you want and what you need. Your needs are things like food to eat, a place to live, and clothing to wear. The things you want would be things like a new phone, vacations, and the occasional Starbucks drink. You don't really need these things, but they are definitely nice to have. When you are an adult, you'll have many expenses. You will need to decide what are the most important things for you to spend your money on and what is least important. The things you need to survive will always be the most important things for you to spend your money on.

Once you have all of your needs sorted out, you can then focus on spending your money on a few things you want.

When you are managing your own money and purchasing your own items, you will be able to see what is most important to you and what really isn't. This helps you to prioritize and learn about finances so that you are completely prepared for the most important things. It also helps you to see how the smaller things in life don't really matter as much.

Financial Independence

At some point, you are going to be financially independent. This means that you have to handle all your finances by yourself. Most people are just thrown into the deep end when they become adults and move out of their parent's home. This is why you find tons of young people getting themselves into debt and ending up in bad financial situations. It's not because they are bad people; they just didn't have the knowledge needed to manage their finances properly.

If you learn how to manage your finances at a young age, it is so much better. You have all your needs taken care of by your parents, so they are your safety net. You have a safe place to learn about your finances and make some mistakes if you need to. It's a lot less pressure, and you will be ready for adulthood.

Avoiding Debt

Debt is probably something you are not all too familiar with. This is actually a good thing because these days, debt is so common, and people tend to struggle with it. Debt is when you owe the bank or another financial service provider money because you borrowed from them. You can borrow in the form of a loan or by using a credit card. When you borrow this money, they put an interest rate on it, so you have to pay back more than what you borrowed. If you are not able to handle credit or loans properly, then this could get you into a very sticky situation. Some people end up in hundreds of thousands of dollars of debt. The number keeps increasing because of the interest they owe. It's not that taking out credit is a bad thing, but you definitely need to know how to use it.

Dodge the Scammers

There are so many scams out there, and it's only getting worse. Online scams are the most common, and since you're probably online all the time, you definitely will be faced with a scam or two at some point. Scammers try to get your information so they can steal or misuse your money or account. The scammers have gotten so good that most people don't even know they are scammed until it is too late. All you have to do is accidentally click on the wrong link, and all your information could be gone. This is why it's so important to never fill out your personal information unless you are 100% sure of who is sending the request. Most banks and other financial service providers do not request you to put in your account information and passwords on emails and other types of communication. It's better to be safe than sorry. It is also wise to call your bank with the phone number they gave you to verify with them that the message or phone call you received is true. Never use the phone number in the message if you think it's a scam.

There are also other ways that someone can get scammed out of the money. This can happen in the real world and is not limited to online. For example, someone might be offering you an item at an escalated price so they can make more profit. You would be buying something that you could get from someone else for much cheaper; this will result in your losing out. Being savvy with your money also means doing research on the things you want to buy for yourself. This way, you know what the going prices are, so you are not scammed when you are trying to purchase something.

You Get a Head Start on Your Future

When you are a teenager, there's a lot of thinking about what you're going to be when you grow up. Your whole life is planning for your future, but the truth is the future is closer than you might think. One day you'll open your eyes, and you will be in your mid-20s and need all the skills necessary to build financial success. The earlier you start building the skills, the better it's going to be for you. You will have a lot of practice by the time you hit adulthood, and you will be able to trust yourself to make the right decisions.

BASIC FINANCIAL CONCEPTS AND TERMINOLOGY

One of the biggest reasons finances seem so difficult to understand is that there are a lot of difficult words and terms that are used. These can seem overwhelming, but it's just because you're not familiar with them yet. The more you start seeing these words and understanding them in context, the more you will understand other types of financial concepts. Below are some of the most common financial concepts and terminology. This should help you understand the book a lot better.

Savings Account: This is where you will save your money for future use or for specific items. If you earn a salary, have it deposited into a savings account. It is best to transfer the money you need from your savings into your checking. Keep in mind you may be required to maintain a minimum amount in your checking account. Many savings accounts also have higher interest rates, so you can gain interest while you leave your money in the account.

Checking Account: This is a transactional bank account. It is easy for you to access your money and pay for things, so you can use it whenever you want. Just keep in mind to never write a check for more money than is in this account, or the check will "bounce," and you will be charged a fee.

Bounced Check: This is a check you write for which there is not enough money in your checking account to cover the purchase price. The bank does not approve the transfer of money, and the check "bounces" back to the account holder. Then the account holder will likely be charged a penalty fee for non-sufficient funds (NSF).

Debit Card: This allows you to have access to the money in your account. You will only be able to spend what is in the account, so always make sure you have enough otherwise, your purchase will be declined.

Interest: This is a percentage that a lender charges the borrower for borrowing money. You can either gain interest or owe interest. If you put your money in an investment or in a savings account, you will be earning interest. If you borrow money, take out a loan, or are using credit, then you will owe back interest.

Loan: This is when you borrow money at a specific interest rate. You will need to pay back the money by a specified date.

Credit Card: This is a specific type of loan where you get a card and can spend an agreed-upon amount of money each month. You also have to agree to pay back a minimum amount each month. This is called revolving credit, as you keep getting a renewed amount each month as long as you are paying back the minimum. An interest rate is also imposed upon you, so the longer you do not pay off the full amount, the more interest you will owe back.

Credit Score: This is how banks and other financial service providers can tell whether you are good with debt and credit or not. Your credit score is worked out based on your history, current debt, how much available credit you have, the length of credit and loans, as well as a few other factors.

Investment: This is an asset that will hopefully generate income for you or increase in value over time.

Stock: This is a piece or a share of a company that you can purchase on the stock market. This way, the company can raise funds in order to expand and grow. As the company expands, the value of the stock will increase, and you will be able to sell your share for more money than you purchased it.

Bond: This is a way for corporations and governments to raise more money for themselves. You are essentially loaning them money, and they will pay you back a specified interest rate. The bond is locked in for a certain amount of time, and once the time has elapsed, you will get back the original money invested and the interest earned.

Inflation: This refers to the overall increase in price for services and goods. The cost of living increases over time, so you cannot purchase items for the same price as you did a few years ago.

Taxes: This is a portion of your income that you are required to pay to governments (federal, state, county, city) in order for them to fund government-based services and activities. This can include running public schools, military operations, and maintaining public spaces.

SETTING FINANCIAL GOALS

Most people set goals and don't even realize it. A goal is something you want in the future, and then you make a plan to get it. Even saying that you want a new pair of sneakers could be a goal. You might not be able to afford them right now, but you can save toward them until you have enough money to buy them. Being able to set financial goals throughout your life is so important. It helps you to put your money to work and create good money habits. In order to reach your financial goals, you will need to be disciplined in the way you handle your money and make sure the habits you have in place will help you to reach your end goal.

There are many different categories when it comes to financial goals. These usually indicate how long it will take for you to get there. Short, medium, and long-term goals all need different strategies in order to get to the end. A short-term goal is something you can accomplish in a few months to a year. A new pair of sneakers would be a short-term goal. A medium-term goal will probably take you between 1 to 5 years to accomplish. Things like a down payment on a property, an overseas vacation, or a wedding could fall into this category. Then we have the long-term goals, which will take you more than 5 years to accomplish. One of the most common long-term goals is to save enough money to have a comfortable retirement.

You can have multiple different goals running at the same time. However, it is important that you track all of your goals and understand where your money is going. You don't want to overcomplicate things or overcommit yourself to too many goals because then it becomes difficult to reach any of them. It's important to understand how much money you have and how much each financial goal is going to cost you. This way, you can better plan and prepare for all of it.

Start Small

If you have never actively set goals before, how you start is going to be incredibly important. It is always better to start with a small goal so you can get the hang of it. If you set a goal that is too big and too far off, it might be difficult to stick to the plan. Once you start reaching the smaller goals, you will gain the confidence to set bigger ones and will have a higher chance of actually reaching them. When a baby starts learning how to walk, they don't sign up for a marathon. Small baby steps first, then they learn how to get faster as they grow. The same principle applies here.

Your small goals can be anything related to finances. You can decide you want to open up a savings account, save $100 for an item of clothing, or commit to writing out a budget. These are all small things that shouldn't take up that much time, and once you have reached those goals, you'll feel a lot more motivated to start planning other goals to reach.

Weigh the Costs and Benefits

Being able to reach your goals will come at a cost. This may not be a monetary cost; it could also be your time and your energy. Being able to think through every goal you set is going to be crucial so you can set the right ones. Let's say you want to be an actor or on Broadway when you are older. This is something you are super passionate about, so your plan is to take steps toward that long-term goal. You hear about an acting camp that is taking place over the summer. They are bringing in some amazing and talented actors to speak to the campers and help them to hone their skills and build connections. This would be an amazing opportunity, and it's something you really want to do.

There is a cost to go to this camp. Firstly, you will need to have the money to pay for the camp itself as well as spending money for when you get there. You will also be giving up most of your summer and won't be able to spend time with your friends and family. Before hearing about this camp, you were planning on getting a summer job to earn some extra cash, but now that you want to go to this camp, it's going to be taking up all of your time, and you won't be able to get the job. With all of this information in mind, you have to ask yourself whether or not the camp is actually worth it. Does the cost of going to the camp over the summer match the benefits you will be getting? For every person, the answer to this question will probably be different. It is important to understand where you stand so you can decide whether or not this camp is a good idea.

With any financial goal, it helps if you write down the pros and cons. Write down what you need in order to fulfill the goal and what you will be giving up in order to reach it. You can also highlight some of the benefits that will come from reaching the goal. All of this will help you to decide whether the goal is worth it or not. Remember, a goal might not seem worth it right now, but it could totally be worth it in the future. While you may not be able to reach it at this point in your life, you can save the goal and re-look at it at another point in time.

SMART Goals

A great method for goal setting is SMART goals. Each letter stands for a specific part of the method. Every goal you set should be specific, measurable, achievable, realistic, and time-bound. If you look at every goal through this lens, you will be able to set goals that you can achieve. Many people set very basic goals, and it doesn't actually help them come up with a plan. For example, if you want to be rich one day, this isn't a good goal. It is way too vague, and you can't see the steps in order to get there.

You can use this as an inspiration to set your goals. Instead of it being so vague, you can say you want to be in a high-paying job by the time you are 30 and have $20,000 in your savings account. This is way more specific, and you can plan to reach the goal. You will be able to look at different job opportunities and see which ones are going to be the highest paying. Then you can see what the requirements are for these jobs. Once you graduate high school, you can go to college and study for a degree that will put you in line for the career path needed. You can then start saving toward the goal by budgeting correctly and making sure you are not blowing all of your money.

This example is a long-term goal, but you can do it with short-term goals as well. Once you have written down a goal, go back and ask yourself those five questions. Is it specific? Is it measurable? Is it achievable? Is it realistic? Does it have a timeframe or due date? All of these things are going to help you set goals that are more easily achieved.

IN REAL LIFE

Sarah had graduated college about two years ago, but in order to graduate, she had to take out a financial aid loan for $20,000 at 7%. After graduation, she got a great job but still continues to pay for the $20,000 debt she incurred, which continues to grow at 7% annually. At this point, Sarah is feeling completely overwhelmed because this is not the plan she had for herself. Being in debt is holding her back from her other financial goals and from being able to live freely.

She knows that she needs a plan in order to pay off her debt. Otherwise, she's never going to be able to live the life she wants. What she needs is a budget. Not knowing where her money is going and how it is working means that she can't actually put together a plan to pay off her debt. Building a budget will allow her to see how much money is coming into her account and how much is leaving. Then she will be able to set financial goals based on how much money she has. She already knows that the number one thing she needs to do is pay off her debt. Once that is done, she can start saving toward things like traveling or buying a property.

She takes all of her debt statements and sees how much she actually owes. Then she looks at how much money she needs to pay in order to pay off the minimum each month. If she's going to keep paying the minimum, she will never get rid of the debt. Debt is sneaky like that. They always tell you that you only have to pay off the minimum, but the truth is that if you do that, you will pay way much more than the original debt. Instead, you keep having to pay back interest for the rest of your life. The only way she can get out of debt is to pay back as much as possible.

When Sarah wrote down all of her expenses, she realized that she spent quite a bit of money on her daily Starbucks drink. On top of that, she eats out about three times a week. Even though she loves going out to eat and can't live without coffee, she decided she was going to cut out these things for the next year. Instead, she would make her coffee at home and try new recipes. This frees up a lot of extra money that she pays toward her debt. Now she is able to pay back more than the minimum and is quickly paying off her debt. All she needed was a plan and a goal. When she had that, everything started falling into place and working for her.

The thing that really helped Sarah was creating a budget. A budget is a powerful tool that helps you to plan and see where your money is going. In the next chapter, we are going to dive deeper into creating a budget so that you can have full control over your money. I know you might be thinking that you don't even have a job and don't have that much money to budget with anyway. Even if you just earn $10 a month, it is still a good idea to have a budget. Remember, you are building a habit, so any small amount of money counts as income.

2

STRATEGY 1—CREATING A BUDGET AND MANAGING EXPENSES

"Budgeting is not just for people who do not have enough money. It is for everyone who wants to ensure that their money is enough."

— ROSETTE MUGIDDE WAMAMBE

Imagine you purchased a brand new desk. You've been eyeing this piece of furniture for a long time, and it just went on sale, so you quickly clicked "add to cart." Now you have your dream workstation ready to go, and you know it's going to help you be so much more productive. When the pack is delivered to your home, you realize that it doesn't come with any instructions on how to build it. It seems easy enough to put together, so you decide you're just going to do it yourself. After about an hour and a half of work, the desk looks pretty good. There are a few screws left over, but you have no idea where those go, so you just ignore them. The desk seems sturdy enough, so maybe they're just extras.

You decide to put all your stationery and supplies on your desk and set everything up. The next day you get home from school, and you plop your backpack on the desk and hear a crash. The whole desk has collapsed! Even though it looks good from the outside, there was something going on that wasn't working. Your desk wasn't as strong as it looked, and now it has caused some damage, and you need to start all the way from the beginning. It would've been so much easier if you had the instructions.

You might be thinking, what does this have to do with managing your finances or budgeting? Well, budgeting is just like creating a blueprint for your finances. You create instructions and a plan, so you have full control of your money. This will help you to create a strong foundation for your finances so it doesn't collapse later on. This way, you're not going to be stressed out about money or run out in the middle of the month. Even though it might take a little bit longer to work on a budget, it is definitely worth it.

UNDERSTANDING YOUR INCOME AND EXPENSES

Before you can start working on your budget, you need to know what you are working with. This means you have to have a good idea of your income and your expenses. Your income is everything that comes into your bank account or is given to you in cash. This could be money earned from a part-time job, your allowance money, or money that has been given to you as a gift. It is a good idea to write all of the various forms of income you have and how much you make each month. Now you know exactly what you're working with and how much you can budget for.

Step two in the process is to figure out what your main expenses are. There are probably a few things that you have to spend your money on each month. When you are older, you will have bills that you will be paying for, and this is a necessity each month. Things like utilities, rent, and insurance will be coming out of your account every month. This makes it very easy to plan for it. You probably don't have any of these expenses right now, but you might have a few things like your Spotify or Apple Music account or you know you spend $50 per month on transport to get to your sports club. Whatever your expenses are each month, make a list and write down how much you are spending.

Once you know what your income is and what your expenses are, then you can find out the difference. Subtract your expenses from your income and see how much money you have left. If you realize that you don't have any money left this means you are probably misusing your money in some way. Right now, you might be asking your parents for a little extra when you run out, but this could set you up for creating a bad habit. When you are an adult, and you want to purchase something that you don't have the money for, you will have to take out debt. It might seem like a small amount at the moment, but it can really add up. It is always better to make sure your spending matches or is less than your income.

CREATING A BUDGET

Now that you have the base layer for your budget, you can start working on creating a detailed plan for your money. You can use a spreadsheet on your phone or computer, or you can do it old school with a pen and paper. It doesn't really matter; you just have to pick the method that will work best for you. There are also some amazing budgeting apps that you can download. One of the most popular ones is called Mint. Some of these apps do come with a fee, so make sure you understand that because it will be an expense that you will need to add to your budget.

You already have a list of expenses written out, but sometimes this doesn't reflect your true spending. The truth is that most of us are really bad at estimating how much we are spending. The best way to get a good idea of how much you spend each week and each month is to track it. In order to do this, you will need to have a notepad or a spreadsheet that you fill in every time you spend money. Even if you buy something for a few cents, you will need to write it down. Write down what you spent the money on and how much it costs you. At the end of the week or the month, you can add everything up and see how much you are truly spending. It might actually surprise you how much money you're spending on things that might not be as important. There are also many good spending tracker apps that you can download.

You can start categorizing you're spending so you know where your weak spots are. We all have weak spots when it comes to spending money. These are things that we just love to buy or spend money on, even if we don't need them. Some people spend a lot of money on snacks and candy. Others will spend it on mods for games. Some people prefer spending money on clothing and accessories. If you know where most of your unnecessary spending is coming from, then you can pay attention to those areas and avoid them as much as possible.

Tracking your spending is something that's going to take at least a few weeks. This will give you the best idea of how you spend your money. Track your spending for a few weeks, and then you can move on to the next step of creating a budget. This is where you look at your spending and see what is important and what is not important. One of the most important things you can do with your money is save it for the future. Having an emergency fund, investing, and saving for important financial goals is essential. Since you have already worked out a few of your financial goals, you can take that into account when you are budgeting. Decide how much you are going to save toward each of your goals every month. These will be your priorities because they are very important to you.

Since you know what is most important to you and what is least important, you can start cutting out the things that are least important to make more room for the important stuff. This might mean that you have to cut down on buying soda from the vending machine at school every day or only buy one upgrade for your video games each month rather than two or three. These small cutbacks will help you to free up extra money so you can do the things you really want to.

It is also important to remember that not every month is going to look the same. There will be some months when you have extra money and some when you might need to cut back a bit more. If you have a friend or family member who has a birthday this month, then you are going to need to save up more money to buy them a present. In a month when there is no special event, you might have more money to spend on yourself. This is why it is so important to look at your budget every month. Plan for whatever is happening in that month and adjust accordingly. It is going to take some time to get used to doing this, but after a few budgeting cycles, you will start to realize how your money works. It will get a lot easier to budget, and the time you spend budgeting will get shorter.

TIPS FOR REDUCING EXPENSES

Now that you have your budget written out, it is time to start looking for ways you can reduce your spending. Believe it or not, we all tend to spend way more money than we actually need to. We live in a world that pushes content and consumerism at us all the time. Scrolling through TikTok, you see dozens of influencers showing us the new gadget they bought or reviewing brand-new clothing items. It becomes very difficult not to want those things. This means we end up spending a lot more than we should, and it becomes difficult to reach financial goals that are important to us. This is why knowing a few saving hacks could be super helpful.

Keep an Eye on Subscriptions

Overtime subscriptions can really pile up. You might need a subscription to something for a short time, but forget that you even signed up in the first place. I remember a few years ago, I was going through my subscriptions and realized I had over eight subscriptions that I was paying for, but I wasn't even using them. Sure, I needed it at the time, but eventually, they became redundant. Now I was paying for something that didn't have any benefit to me anymore.

This is why it's important to keep track of your subscriptions. Maybe you signed up for Google Cloud but don't need it anymore because you also have a subscription to iCloud. Do you really need that many cloud services? Every time you sign up for a subscription, write it down and write down how much you are paying for it. You can make this a section in your budget. Then you always know exactly what subscriptions you are signed up for, and when you no longer need it, you can go and cancel it.

We Have Food at Home

Parents love to tell their children that they can't eat out because there's food at home. This can be incredibly frustrating when you are a teenager, but when you have to spend your own money on food, it starts to make sense. Eating out all the time really does take up a lot of your money. Cooking at home is a lot cheaper because you can buy a lot more ingredients and cook multiple meals.

Since you are probably still living with your parents or a guardian, they will be taking care of all your food needs. You don't really need to buy your own food, and any food you do buy, it's just because you feel like it, not because you're actually starving. Telling yourself that you have food at home will help you to save a ton of money. This doesn't mean that you can't eat out once in a while; just make sure it doesn't turn into a habit.

Make a Checklist

Impulse buying is a real trap. This happens when you see something that looks really cool, and you want to buy it immediately. I'm sure you have bought quite a few things that aren't being used right now. Every home has a junk drawer where everyone puts the random stuff they bought but never use. This could've been money saved for something more important.

The best thing you can do when it comes to spending is plan. If you see something that you really want to buy, write it down on a list. I have a list on my notes app, and when I go out to the store, I only allow myself to buy things that are on that list. This could be clothing, shoes, technology, or literally anything else. If I notice that I need another jacket for winter, I will put it on the list. When I'm going to go shopping, I will specifically look for that winter jacket. I might come across some other items of clothing that look really nice, but because it's not on my list, I will avoid buying it. This way, I stick to the plan and make sure I only spend money on things that I actually need and are important.

If you are at the stage where you are buying your own groceries or helping your parents buy groceries, make sure you have a list. Throughout the month, as things get finished, you can add them to the shopping list. Then at the end of the month, you know what you need. You won't be tempted to buy something because it's on sale or because it just looks cool. This also helps to prevent food waste because you only have the items that you're actually going to use.

Use Cash Over Card

Sometimes, it's a lot easier to save money and spend wisely when you're using cash. This is because you can feel the physical money in your hand, and you can see it going away when you pay for something. When you just swipe or scan your card, you can't really see the money being deducted from the account, so it doesn't feel that bad. Only when you go back and check your account will you notice that you have less money.

Using physical money also helps you to spend less and stick to your budget because you only have a limited amount. You won't have access to all the money in your account. If you are going out somewhere or going to spend your money, you can withdraw the amount in cash. This way, you know exactly how much you are spending and what you have left. It will be a lot easier to plan and stay on budget.

Choose Cheaper Activities

We all want to go out and have fun with our friends, but sometimes these activities can get pretty pricey. If your friends always want to do things that are on the expensive side, it might help to start suggesting activities that are cheaper. You don't have to pay an arm or leg to have fun.

Let's say your friends want to go to the movies. These days going to the movies can cost a lot of money. You aren't just paying for the movie ticket but also the snacks and food you'll be eating when you get there. You could suggest having a movie night at your house. Everyone can bring their favorite snacks, and you can sit in your living room in your pajamas. It's a lot more comfortable, you will have a lot more snacks, and you can watch more than one movie.

There are always ways you can choose a cheaper activity. It might just be a case of doing some research and finding a similar activity at a cheaper price. Maybe there could even be a deal for large groups, and you can invite more people in order to cut down on the price. You don't have to do this all the time, but if there is a way to spend less money, then you should definitely go for it.

STICKING TO YOUR BUDGET

Now that you have your budget all written out and you have figured out some ways to reduce your spending. You have to focus on sticking to the budget. Just because you have a budget doesn't mean that it's going to be easy to follow it all the time. You will probably be tempted to spend a bit more here and there, and this could lead you to go way over budget. Thankfully, there are a few things you can do to help rein in your spending and stick to your budget.

Give It a Day

Most of the useless things we buy are a result of impulse spending. Even if we have a certain amount in our budget for something like clothing, we can still end up buying something we regret. Instead of simply buying something because you saw it and you liked it, take some time to think about it.

When you see something you like, the emotions rise up in your body and make you want to buy it. This means you are buying some things based on emotions and not using logic. Most of the time, finances are all about logic. Taking a day or two to pause and think about it is going to help you.

Budget to Zero

There are many different ways to budget, and most people choose to budget based on category. If you struggle to stick to a budget, you can try budgeting to zero. This is when all your expenses and your income are exactly the same. Instead of leaving some money spare, you make sure that every dollar is doing something in your budget.

This doesn't mean that you have to spend every single dollar on something. Budgeting to zero also takes into account you're saving and investing. It just helps you to ensure that your money is doing something productive and that you aren't wasting any leftover money.

The No-Spend Challenge

If you are someone who loves a challenge, why not try a no-spend challenge? This is when you decide not to spend any money for a certain amount of time. People usually do this for a few weeks or a month. If you have important things to pay for, like subscriptions or bills, these will still need to be taken care of. The no-spend challenge is more about not spending your money on things you don't need. You won't buy any new clothes or any unnecessary food items or even spend on fun activities. Doing this helps you to see that you can actually survive if you're not spending your money, and it helps you to save a huge chunk toward your goals.

Meal Planning

Planning out your meals is a great addition to grocery shopping. If you plan out your meals for the week, then you'll know exactly what ingredients you need to make that meal. This means you only buy exactly what you need, and it really helps you to cut down on how much you spend at the grocery store. You will also cut down on food waste because you will not be buying anything unnecessary. It also makes sure that you always have food available so you're not tempted to order takeout.

Shop Online

Buying groceries online and online shopping, in general, can actually help you save money. This is only if you do it smartly. When you purchase things online, you only have certain items in front of you. You have to search for the items you want, and those are what will be pulled up. This way, you only buy what you need and aren't tempted by aisles and rows of other items. You are less likely to see other things you might want because you are just focused on the things you need. If you are going to shop online, make sure that you don't scroll endlessly on the stores' pages. Know what you are planning on buying and only search for those items.

Pay Yourself First

Paying yourself first is the concept of saving your money before you spend it on anything else. Many people spend money first and then save whatever is left over. This isn't a good plan because you are not prioritizing yourself and your goals. Instead, plan on saving first and then use the rest of your money toward other things. Remember to save your money in a separate bank account from your regular checking or transactional bank account. If it is out of your regular bank account, you'll feel less tempted to use it. A great plan is to decide that 10% of all you earn is yours to keep.

Compare Before Committing

It is a good idea to compare different stores and different items so you can find the cheapest option. This can actually help you save a lot of money because some stores will have sales on certain items while others don't. Simply taking the time to research the item you want to buy and looking for cheaper options will help you to save so much money.

DO IT YOURSELF

Now is the time for you to create your own budget and do it yourself. Creating a budget can be a trial-and-error experience. You will get a lot better with it as you learn more about your spending habits. The main goal is to get started and commit to doing a budget every month. This will help you to create a habit, and once this is set in stone, things will be a lot easier for you.

- Write down your total income for the month.
- Make a list of your expenses and add them up to get the total.
- Track your spending to find out what you actually spend. Find your weak spots.
- Make a list of your priorities and goals, and write down how much you want to spend on each.

- See how much money you have left over.
- With the leftover money, put it toward other things you might want during the month.
- Look at your budget each week and adjust if needed.
- Repeat!

Budgeting Template:

Income:

Income Source	Planned Amount	Actual Amount
Totals		

Expenses:

Expense Name	Planned Amount	Actual Amount	Left Over
Totals			

Savings:

Savings Name	Amount Saved
Total	

3

STRATEGY 2—SAVING AND INVESTING FOR THE FUTURE

Being able to invest is a great way to grow your wealth. Investing in the stock market is risky, but if you know what you are doing, it's a great place to try to grow your investment because you can get a high amount of returns. About 56% of Americans own stocks and 92% of the highest-income families own stocks (Financial Samurai, 2021). This shows that people see the value in investing in stocks. Many people believe that you need to be earning a lot of money in order to start investing, but that is not the truth. You can start investing with a small amount of money.

THE BENEFITS OF SAVING EARLY

If you are planning on starting to invest, it is always good to start saving first. Building a savings habit is the first step to investing. You might not feel it now, but not having enough money in your savings does come with a lot of stress. As an adult, there could be many different types of situations that pop up and result in you not having enough money for something. If there is an emergency that you have to deal with, you might need to take out a loan or use your credit card in order to pay for it. This can put you in debt and can stress you out. In life, we can never plan and prepare for everything, so it is always good to have a little extra money to use when you need it.

Saving money also helps you to work toward long-term goals. Some of the things you might want in your life are going to be more expensive than you can afford in one month. If you have already built the habit of saving, then saving toward your goals is going to be a lot easier for you.

Learning how to save as young as possible is essential. If you are used to using up your entire salary for the things you want now, then it's going to be very difficult for you to learn how to save later on. However, if you start saving early on in your life, it will already be a habit for you. You will already have savings in your budget, and it's not going to be a huge stress for you to start cutting down on your spending. Saving is a lifestyle, and it is well worth it.

It is good to think of saving as paying yourself first. When you are buying items and spending your money, you are essentially putting money in other people's pockets. This means that other people are profiting from the money that you spend. This doesn't really have much benefit to you and your future. Paying yourself first means that you think of your future before you think of putting money into other people's pockets. When you save, the money goes directly back into your pocket, and you get to grow your savings with any amount of money you have. Most savings accounts will allow you to earn interest, and this means that you can make extra money just by saving. It is always a good idea to look at the interest rate so you know how much your money is going to grow over time.

If you are saving in an account that grows with compound interest, you will be making a lot more money. Compound interest is the type of interest that you earn based on the amount in your account. This means that you can earn interest on top of interest. Let's say you deposit $100 into a compound interest savings or investment account. The interest you will earn is 5%. After the first month, you will have $105. The following month you will have $110.25. The next time your interest is compounded, you will have $115.51. This will keep growing, and eventually, you will start making a lot of money very quickly. The more time you let your money grow, the more money you will have in the end. This is why it is so important to save and invest as early as possible. You don't have to start with a huge amount of money. It's just important that you start somewhere.

This may sound like a great thing, but when you look at how compound interest increases your money, you might think a bit differently. In comparison to simple interest, if you deposited that $100,000 into an account earning 6% annually that uses compound interest, you would have $179,085 at the end of the 10 years. The difference in total earned is more than $20,000 just by compounding the interest. Let's look at the chart below to compare the growth over time.

	Simple Interest (6%)	Compound Interest (6%)
10 years	$160,000	$179,085
20 years	$220,000	$320,713
30 years	$280,000	$574,349
40 years	$340,000	$1,028,572
50 years	$400,000	$1,842,015

Do you see the power of compound interest? There is a massive difference in the amount you make through compound interest than through simple interest. Not only that, but time also works for you when you invest with compound interest. The longer you leave your money to grow, the faster it will increase. In the last ten years, between 40 and 50 years, the amount almost doubled! The sooner you start taking advantage of compound interest, the better it will be for you.

When you make saving a priority, it helps you to avoid getting into debt. Because you already have the money available, you don't have to borrow it from anyone else and can buy the things that you want or need. This helps you to be a lot more financially independent, and you don't have to rely on banks or get loans in order to purchase the things that are important to you. It is also a lot more satisfying when you work toward a goal you really want. Saving allows you to work toward your goals in a healthy and sustainable way.

THE "PAY YOURSELF FIRST" PRINCIPLE

Acquiring wealth is no secret. It is practical and simple. However, it does take discipline, and it is a good habit.

The very first thing to begin to acquire wealth is to pay yourself 10% out of all your income. For example, if you receive $100 in income each week, you would put $10 in your savings drawer, and then you live off the $90 you have left. Eventually, your savings drawer will begin to get full. Imagine at the end of a year (52 weeks) you will have $520, 2 years $1,040 plus the interest that money is earning.

The odd thing, which I myself do not really understand, is that I continued to manage all my bills just as well with $90. When you first start saving 10%, it may seem difficult, and you might think you need that money for other things. However, in reality, you won't even miss it, and you'll still be able to handle your bills and expenses just fine. The great thing is, as time goes on, you'll notice your savings drawer filling up, which will make you happy, confident, and empowered.

It depends on you and what you desire the most. Do you desire instant gratification each day, such as; jewelry, clothes, more food, things that are quickly gone and forgotten, or do you have your sights on something more substantial, land or investments that provide income? The goal is to save enough money in order to put that money to work for you.

The concept described is known as the "Pay Yourself First" principle, and it's a powerful strategy for wealth accumulation. By setting aside a portion of your income (in this case, 10%) before spending on your expenses, you prioritize saving and building wealth. Do you think the money you earn is yours to keep? If you have a house or apartment, don't you have to pay for rent, food, and utilities?

The key is to prioritize yourself and your financial future by setting aside money first. By living on a little less and saving consistently, you'll start building wealth even if you get a weekly allowance. This approach teaches you how to manage your money wisely and make choices that bring long-term benefits and security. So, consider saving 10% of your income to unlock a brighter financial future for yourself.

Let's say you have been saving for 12 weeks now, and you just got paid your thirteenth payment of $100; you put $90 in your spending jar and $10 into your savings jar, which now has $130. Now you want to buy that new video game that costs $50. You still take the $50 from your spending jar, which leaves you $40 for other things. Meanwhile, your savings jar is still growing. Your good habits and discipline are evident.

By saving 10% consistently, you develop discipline and patience and learn to manage your money wisely. You'll find that you can still take care of your bills, buy things you need, and enjoy activities with your friends, with some sacrifices, all while building up your savings. It's like having the best of both worlds—enjoying the present and securing your future.

Remember, it's about making choices that align with what matters most to you. While it might be tempting to spend all your money on immediate wants, setting aside 10% helps you prioritize your long-term dreams and aspirations.

So, start small by saving a portion of your income each time you receive income. As your savings grow, you'll feel more confident and empowered about your financial future, knowing that you're taking steps toward building wealth.

TYPES OF SAVINGS ACCOUNTS AND INVESTMENTS

When you are getting into saving and investing, you will have tons of options. This might seem very overwhelming because you don't know which one to choose. This is why we are going to go through the different types of savings and investment accounts. There are many different types, and they suit different people. You definitely don't have to have all of them, but it's always good to do your research to make sure you're choosing the right one.

Traditional Savings Account

The first account is the most basic, and it's a traditional savings account. This is a great starting point if you haven't saved or invested before. It will help you to build up the habit and allow you to save for short-term goals. You will be able to open up a savings account with your bank, and this will be an account that is separate from your credit or checking account.

With a savings account, you will be able to earn some interest. This interest is usually not a high amount, so you shouldn't expect massive returns. You are usually allowed to make withdrawals from your savings account, but this might be limited, so check with your bank. A traditional savings account is a great way to save your money, but you also have access to it when you need it. When you need more money, transfer it from your savings to your checking account.

High-Yield Savings

A high-yield savings account basically works the same as a traditional savings account, but the interest you will be earning is higher. This means that your money will grow faster in this type of account. Because it is almost the same as a traditional savings account, you will not need a huge deposit in order to open the account. This means almost anyone can have a high-yield savings account, but not all banks offer this, so make sure you check before signing up.

MMA

This stands for Money Market Account. This may not be good for beginners because you need to have a specific amount of funds in order to put your money here. People who have large amounts of money that they want to keep safe can choose this account because it is insured for up to $250,000. This makes it a lot safer to save large sums of money and will give the investor some peace of mind. Not only that, but there is a higher interest rate with this type of account.

CDs

I'm not talking about how people in the early 2000s listened to music! A CD stands for Certificate of Deposit. If you have a very specific goal that you're trying to reach and you have a specific date you want to reach by, this is a great option. These types of accounts will pay you back with a higher interest rate because you are committing to leaving your money in the account for a specific amount of time. It is a great option if you have a financial goal in mind and you want to reach it in a few years. Just keep in mind whatever money you place in a CD, you will not have access to it for the length of its life. Most people use CDs for money they know they are not going to need. For example, you inherit $1,000 when you're in 6th grade; you don't need the money until you start college. You can put the money in an MMA or in a CD, depending on which one will give you the most interest.

Stocks

I've already mentioned stocks a bit earlier in the book, but let's dive into a bit more detail. When you buy an individual stock, you are buying a piece of a company. This makes you a partial owner, but because it is such a small piece, you do not have control over what happens in the company. There are large shareholders who do have control over the decisions made in the company, and these people will sit on the board. A company can choose to put its stock on the market so they are able to raise more funds to continue growing the business.

We call it the stock market because you can buy and sell your stocks in order to make a profit or to get what you want. The goal is to buy a stock at a cheaper price and then wait for the company to grow so you are able to sell your stock at a higher price. So, you buy it for less money and sell it for more. This is the most common way to make money from an individual stock. It is important to do your research when it comes to investing in stocks so you know whether or not it is a good company to put your money in. This is why stocks can be very risky, and you could lose all your money if you pick a losing company.

There is always going to be a risk when you are investing in the stock market because it can be difficult to predict how it's going to go. There are many different factors that come into play when discussing the price of stocks. Even if a company is really successful, the price of the stock could go down because the industry the company falls under is doing badly. Other reasons a stock might decrease in price is an economic issue or even if there is a change in the leadership of the company. As soon as people feel it's not safe to invest in a specific company, they will start pulling out their money, and this will cause the price of the stock to go down.

The stock market is a pretty volatile market, and this means the prices go up and down all the time. Throughout the day, the price of a specific stock could fluctuate hundreds of times. This is why many investors say it is best to purchase stocks and hold them. This means that you wait out any downturns and low prices because, eventually, the stock will increase in price again. In general, the stock market has always shown increases 70% of the time, and this is why it's a good investment, as long as you do your research. The stock market is like gambling, but unlike gambling, you are able to research the company you want to invest in to make a good decision.

Another way people can make money through the stock market is by investing in a stock that gives out dividends. When you invest in this type of stock, the owners will pay you a portion of the profit they make every few months. The amount you will get is usually reflected in the amount you invested in the company. Not all companies will give dividends for their stocks, so you should do your research and make sure you are investing in companies that you are comfortable with.

The great thing about the stock market is that you don't have to have a ton of money in order to start investing. There are stocks that are going for super cheap, so you can always start with what you have. Since stocks tend to increase in price over the years, the longer you hold out, the more money you will probably be making. However, it is important to diversify your portfolio. This means you have many different types of investments and stocks in your investment portfolio. This way, if one of the stocks were to take a dive, you would have many other investments that are making money for you. This is a very safe way to invest and definitely, one of the best if you know what you're doing.

Bonds

While the stock market can be quite volatile, and this does make it a risky investment, bonds tend to be a lot safer. When you take out a bond, you are essentially lending money to a company or government. They might need this money for a whole lot of reasons, and in return for the loan, they will pay you back interest on the loan. You have to agree to lock in the bond for a certain amount of time. This means you do not have access to the money you have invested until the time elapses. When the time is up, it is called the maturity date, and that's when you get back the original amount you invested, as well as all the interest you earned.

Even though bonds are safer than stocks, the interest rate is going to be smaller. One thing you do have to keep in mind when it comes to investments is that the more risk you are willing to take, the more potential rewards you will get from it. This doesn't mean you always have to make risky choices with your money, but many of the risky investments do give back a higher interest rate. There are strategies you can put in place to lower the amount of risk you will be facing. This includes diversifying your portfolio with both stocks and bonds. Since stocks are riskier and give you back more money, while bonds are safer, but the interest rate is lower, you can balance out your portfolio with both of these.

Investment Funds

Investing can be a tricky business, and sometimes people don't want to put all the time and effort into managing their investment portfolios. Investing in some sort of fund is a great way to invest and make sure you're getting the most out of your money. When you invest in a fund, you are essentially giving your money to someone else to manage for you. There will be a fund manager who chooses the investments based on your goals and the criteria you have given to them. They will then choose which investments are going to be best suited to you, and you just have to commit to paying the fee as well as the specific amount you want to be invested each month.

In most cases, a fund will give you back a good amount of money because there is a larger amount for the fund manager to play with. It's not just your money that's being invested, but a whole lot of other investors' as well. The fund manager will pool all of the money collected and make investment choices. There are many different funds out there, and they all have their benefits. It is always important to research what funds are available through your bank or other service providers. This way, you have a good idea of how much it's going to cost you and what's going to be best suited for you.

The most common types of funds are mutual funds, index funds, and exchange-traded funds. With a mutual fund, the fund manager will invest in a combination of stocks and bonds. They will diversify your portfolio based on your needs, age, and goals. An index fund works in a similar way, but it's not managed by a fund manager. This means that the fees you pay are going to be less because the fund is basically tracking a specific Index instead of investing individually. An exchange-traded fund or ETF also tracks popular indexes and tries to match the performance. These funds are sold on the stock market. This impacts the fees that you will be paying, and you can choose the amount you are willing to purchase them for. You basically make a profit from how well the overall market grows.

Retirement Plans

Retirement accounts are a great way to save for retirement. Most teenagers aren't really thinking about retirement, but the earlier you think about it and start investing, the more money you will have when you retire. The two most common retirement accounts are IRAs and 401(k)s.

An IRA stands for Individual Retirement Account. There are two types of IRAs, and these are traditional IRAs and Roth IRAs. The difference between both comes down to taxes. With a Roth IRA, you contribute funds on which you've already paid income taxes, commonly referred to as post-tax income. With a traditional IRA, you contribute money that has not yet been taxed, called pre-tax income, which can lower your taxable income level; the IRS gives tax deductions for contributions. Money then grows tax deferred until you take it out at age 59, and the tax will be higher.

A 401(k) is a great retirement account that can only be offered by an employer. This means that you won't be able to open up this type of account on your own. Your employer opens it for you and will also deposit money into this account for you. Some employers choose to match your contributions to the account. So, if you want to invest $200 into your 401(k), your employer will match this, and you won't end up investing $400 into your account each month. This means you can double your investment. Not all employees offer this, so make sure you read your contract to see if it is an option. If your employer does offer matching, you should try your best to max this out. Most employers will contribute up to a certain amount, and if you know what the limit is, you can essentially get as much of this "free money" as possible.

Real Estate

Investing in real estate means that you are investing in property. There are actually two ways to do this. The first one is traditional property investment, where you purchase a physical property, and the other one is called a Real Estate Investment Trust (REIT). We will dive more into this in a later chapter.

TIPS AND TRICKS TO INVEST WISELY

Investing can be daunting because you are putting your money into a resource or assets and hoping that you'll get a good return on it. Investing with knowledge reduces the risk of losing or decreasing your capital. However, the rewards are worth it. Investing is mostly about forming good habits. By following these tips and tricks, you'll definitely see positive results.

Start With a Savings Account

Before you start investing in the stock market or anything fancy, you should start with a savings account. A savings account is going to really help you build the habit of putting money away for the future. It is also important that you have a good amount of money in your savings account before you start investing. Building an emergency fund should be one of your first financial goals.

Investing is a Long-Term Game

Most people want to invest so they can get rich quickly. I can't tell you how many people have tried to do this and ended up losing all the money. When you try to play games with investing, most of the time, you will lose out. Investing is a long-term thing. This means you will be putting money away in your investments and not doing anything with it until many years later. This is usually the best investment strategy because it takes the emotion out of it. If you see the stock market taking a dive and your investments are worth a lot less than you wanted, you might be tempted to pull out all your investments. In a few weeks, the stock market may pick up again, and your investments will be worth a lot more than what they are worth now. Because emotion took over, you have now lost out. This is why having a long-term mindset when it comes to investing is always the best way to go.

Always Do Your Research

Before you make any kind of investment, it is always a good idea to do your research. Understand the type of investment you are making as well as the companies you will be investing in. This is going to help you make smart choices. There are always going to be new investments that pop up, and you might want to give them a go. Taking some time to do some research can help you to think about things logically, and you can invest in something that you truly believe in.

Ask Your Parents to Help Open a Custodial Account

If you think you are ready to start investing in a retirement account, then why not ask your parents to open up a custodial IRA for you? You can open one even if you just have a short-time job because anyone who has an income can open one. This means you can start investing in your retirement from a very young age and will probably have a good amount of money when the time comes for you to retire. It is also a great way to get used to investing and seeing how your money grows over time.

IN REAL LIFE

Luke started getting interested in investing when he was about 13 years old. He was in a math class at school, and his teacher assigned a project to each one of them. Each student had to pick a specific stock on the stock market and write a report on how it performed over time. Most of the students picked very well-known brands, such as Starbucks and Apple, but not Luke. He decided he was going to pick a company that was founded in his hometown. He already knew a little bit about it and thought that it would grow over time.

He started becoming incredibly interested in investing. Even though this was just a project, he started watching how stocks performed in real life. By the time he was 17 years old, he had started trading fake stocks on a website online. This helps many investors to practice investing before they start using real money to invest. These websites just mimic the stock market, so you can play around and get used to investing in stocks. He actually got incredibly good at it, and his parents gave him some money to start investing for real. After about two years, he was able to triple the amount he had initially invested.

Many people believe that you cannot start investing until you are much older, but Luke is proof that you can. He now teaches other teenagers and even adults how to invest in the stock market. He practiced for so long, so he was fully prepared when he had real money to start investing. Even if you don't have any physical money to invest, why not open up a fake investing account online? These accounts allow you to pretend to invest and see how much you can profit from it. This way, when you get older and can invest with your own money, you already know how things work. You can already form a strategy from now and can hit the ground running as soon as possible.

You should never let your age be a barrier to what you can do. Teenagers who start early and think about their future tend to become a lot more successful. You have more time now to try things and see what works for you and what doesn't. This also applies to entrepreneurship and starting your own business. If this is something that you're interested in, you can start working on it starting now. You don't have to wait until you are an adult. That's exactly what we will be diving into in the next chapter.

4

STRATEGY 3—EXPLORING ENTREPRENEURSHIP

Are you the type of person that dreams of doing something they are absolutely passionate about when they're older? Perhaps the thing you are passionate about or that you really want to do isn't even invented yet. Maybe you still want to follow your passions but know it's not going to be a high-paying job. Unless you are choosing a field that is high paying and in demand, you will always have a limit on how much money you can make. Building your own business is one of the best solutions for this.

Being an entrepreneur and starting up your own business is definitely not for everyone. It is a lot harder than working for a company, but the rewards are also greater if you can get it off the ground. If you are passionate about being your own boss and making your own decisions, then this could be a great path for you. This chapter is designed to help you understand what entrepreneurship is and to start thinking about whether it is the right fit for you or not.

WHAT EXACTLY IS ENTREPRENEURSHIP?

At the most basic level, entrepreneurship is being able to build and start up your own business. As the business grows and you put more work into it, it will start to make a profit for you and any partners you have. Some people decide to start a business all on their own, and others work as a group to get it off the ground. Depending on the type of business you want to start and who you have around will dictate whether or not you have partners at the beginning. You might find that other people want to join you in your business as it grows. This means you can start off solo but end up having partners along the way.

Becoming an entrepreneur is definitely a risk. You have to make sure your idea is something that other people want to buy into. Even if you think your idea is the best one ever, other people need to think the same otherwise, you're not going to make a profit. Successful entrepreneurs are people who find a problem and develop a solution for that problem. This could be a product or a service that helps people in a certain way. It doesn't have to be a brand-new innovation, but it does need to offer something that is not currently being offered. If you notice a problem in society, you can be the one that has the solution.

Being an entrepreneur also means a lot of work. Most small businesses end up failing because it takes a lot to get started. You have to remain committed, even when it is hard. The thing is that you never know when you're going to hit your lucky break. Most small business owners tend to bail a lot sooner than they should. This is why it's so important to be resilient when you are a business owner. This will help you persevere through any bad times so you can get the water at the end of it.

There are tons of positives that come with owning your own business. For one, you will be the one in charge, and that means you have a ton of flexibility. You can work whenever you want as long as you are able to do what is necessary for your business. This allows you to have full control over your life and your income. If you are able to run a successful business, you will be able to create more profit and income than if you worked a traditional job. Basically, your earning potential is going to be unlimited. Most people complain about their bosses or the culture of the company, and when you run your own business, you are the boss. You get to set the standard and can run it the way you want to.

With all of these positives, there are also some negative aspects that are important to take into consideration. Starting your own business isn't going to be free. You will need to put in some money in order to get it started. This is why a lot of business owners only start building up their businesses a little later in life. If you are planning to be an entrepreneur, it is a good idea to start planning now. You might need to get a traditional job for a few years so you can save up enough money to build your business. Another thing to take into consideration is that even though you have a lot of flexibility, you also will have to work a lot of hours. This is especially true at the beginning when you are just getting started. You might have to work through the night in order to get things ready and to plan.

When it's your own business, the responsibility is on you to make sure it is successful. If you have employees, they rely on you for their income. This means that you have to do your best for yourself and for the people that work for you. Businesses are always going through ups and downs when it comes to finances. Some months will bring in a whole lot of money, and others will be completely dry. It is your responsibility to make sure there are always finances in the business to pay for what is necessary. This kind of income fluctuation can stress out a lot of people, so it is important to make sure you can handle your finances properly before you start a business.

There are a lot of aspects coming into play when you want to start your own business. You need to be able to think about it clearly. It might be a good idea to talk to somebody who already runs their own business. Ask them questions about how they got to where they are now and tell them to give you a realistic idea of the work they put in. This is not to scare you but prepare you. When the time comes for you to start your own business, you want to have a clear vision of what it's going to take. This way you can actually create a plan that will work.

WHAT DOES A SUCCESSFUL ENTREPRENEUR LOOK LIKE?

Being an entrepreneur is not a one size fits all thing. People of all shapes, sizes, and all backgrounds have been able to start successful businesses. It's not about how much money you have right now or how old you are. It is more about your character and the traits that you possess. Even though entrepreneurs look different, there are certain things that they all possess to help them become successful in any field.

If you don't have these skills right now, you don't have to panic. You can build them into yourself. Be honest and see whether or not these are skills you think you have or skills you can improve on. This will really help you when you start working toward your own business.

A Strong Leader

An entrepreneur is a leader. You will be providing a product or service to other people, and you will have other people working for you. Possessing good leadership skills is essential. When people think of a leader, a lot of people just think of someone who is bossy. Being bossy and being a leader are two completely different things.

A leader is somebody who builds up people and guides them to meet their goals and become successful. A true leader is somebody who cares about other people and wants them to be the best version of themselves. It's also somebody who's not afraid of making decisions and calling the shots. If you find other people always come to you to ask your opinion or for your help, then this is a good indication that you are a natural leader.

Self-Motivated

I think we all know somebody who will never do anything unless they are absolutely forced to. Sure, there's nothing wrong with a bit of encouragement every now and then, but an entrepreneur needs to be self-motivated. There isn't going to be somebody who is motivating you the whole way through. Sometimes it's going to be hard, and you need to tell yourself to do the work even when you don't want to. You need to be motivated by your goals and your passion for your future.

Not Afraid of Failure

You might not want to hear this, but being an entrepreneur means failure. I have not heard of a single business owner or entrepreneur that hasn't failed in their life. In fact, I haven't heard of a single adult who hasn't failed. Failure is a part of life, and it's an even bigger part of owning your own business. This can be very scary for people because nobody really enjoys failing. Can you imagine signing up for a race and expecting to come last? That sounds horrible, and you might think, "Why would you even sign up in the first place?" It is very counterintuitive for us as humans to do things when we know we're going to fail.

When you start a business, you shouldn't expect to fail, but you should be okay with it. Failure is not actually failure unless we give up. It's just a chance for you to learn something new and learn what not to do. The thing with failure is it can make us so scared to even try. This means we don't even give ourselves a chance.

You never know what's going to work or what's not going to work unless you try. You will have to try quite a bit of different things when you have your own business. Some things will work, and others won't. What is most important is you get up and try again.

Innovation

Once you're able to start your own business, the work doesn't stop there. You are going to need to be a person who is always thinking of the next step. Think of huge companies like Microsoft and Apple. We know these companies because they are always innovating. This means they are always creating something new for their customers. Constant improvement in new products that are exciting makes everybody want to know what's going to happen next. They also improve the way they run the companies so they are more efficient. When you are innovative, you always think of new ideas and new ways to do things. This makes your business better and helps you to stay in front of your competition.

Being Okay With Not Knowing

For those of us that don't like asking for help, this is not going to be our favorite thing to hear. With anything in life, we are never going to know everything. This means we need to have other people around us who can help. These are people who we can ask hard questions and get advice from. It's okay to not know something if you are willing to go and ask for help when you need it. Ask for feedback and be willing to listen to what other people have to say. There might be something going on that you haven't even noticed yet. This is why it's so important to have the right people around you because it's going to help you see the bigger picture. Don't be afraid to start those hard discussions.

Good at Networking

This follows on from the previous point. You will find it very difficult to find an entrepreneur that has made it completely on their own. Everybody needs other people around them who will help them and support them. As your business grows, you will need connections, suppliers, people willing to fund you, and business partners. Have you noticed that businesspeople tend to go out on a lot of business lunches and dinners? It might seem very silly and like a waste of time, but during these lunches, they connect with other people and build relationships. This helps them in their businesses because when they need something, they have somebody to call.

Building up a network is essential even if you are an employee at a company. You can get advice and different perspectives from other people. Or you might just need support because you're going through a tough time with your business. Making sure you have the right network around you is essential.

FINDING YOUR PASSION

Finding your passion is a very important part of building the future you want. I'm sure you want to do something that gets you excited when you wake up in the morning. There are a few things that you can do to help you to find your passion, so let's talk about them.

Perspective

The first thing you need to do is believe that you can find something you're passionate about. There are so many different options out there in the world, and chances are you might be passionate about more than one thing. You might also find that you're passionate about something you've never thought of before. This is why it is important to have the perspective that there is good in the world and you will find your passion. If you walk into life with an open mind and optimistic attitude, it will be a lot easier.

What Do You Enjoy?

A passion is something that you actually enjoy doing and something that you care about. One of the easiest ways to find your passion is to look at the things you enjoy. Maybe you have a few hobbies or tasks that you really like to do. Perhaps there's a subject at school that you are really good at and look forward to. Looking at these things that bring you joy and excitement helps you in finding your passion.

Hobby vs. Passion

Even though there might be tons of things you really enjoy doing, not everything can be a job. For example, I love playing with puppies, but there isn't a huge market for a professional puppy petter. Going to the animal shelter and playing with puppies is a hobby because it's something I enjoy doing. However, I can't really turn that into a job that will bring in profit. I might be able to think of other ways to make a profit and still spend time with animals, or I could think of a way to work flexibly so that I can have more time to spend with animals. This way, it's not just a hobby, but I can turn it into a profitable passion. Make sure you draw a clear line between your passions and your hobbies.

It's actually a really good thing to have hobbies because it takes your mind off of work. It allows you to have fun and destress when needed. Every person needs a few hobbies in their life. If you are looking to turn a hobby into a full-time job, you might need to add a few skills to your arsenal to help you. For example, you might be an incredible artist who loves to paint and draw. It can be very difficult to become a world-renowned artist and get your art out there. There is no guarantee that it will be picked up and you can make a profit from it. However, there are plenty of ways to make money through art. For example, there are tons of people who have blogs and websites that need things designed for them. If you become a digital designer or illustrator, you can still be an artist and earn a good amount of money from it. You will just need to learn how to make art digitally and have some tech skills. This way, you can turn a hobby into a job and a business.

Break Down Your Fears

Even if you are incredibly passionate about something, there might always be a little voice at the back of your head that makes you want to back down. We all have this little voice that makes us second-guess ourselves and think that we may not be realistic. If you look at the stories of very famous entrepreneurs, you usually find that they went through their own seasons of doubt. People didn't believe they could be successful with the ideas they had, and if they let this drag them down, then we wouldn't have half the technology and products we have now.

If you ever feel scared to do something, it's actually a good thing. When you are scared or have a little bit of fear, it means that you are going to be doing something important and you are moving forward. It's just the uncertainty that is making the fear pop up and not the fact that you cannot do it. Take some time to think about where the fear comes from and whether or not it is actually legit. In most cases, it's not going to be something you should let hold you back.

Take the First Step

One of my best friends always loved to be prepared, and she loved to plan. When it came time to study for an exam or do a class project, she would have a list of everything she needed to do before she actually sat down and studied. If you walked into a room a few days before an exam, you would notice that it is completely clean and neat. Her desk was spotless, and all her study materials were laid out and filed incredibly neatly. She always said that she needed to plan before she got started. The problem was this was actually just a distraction. She didn't need to clean her entire room and make sure that everything was laid out perfectly. She was just procrastinating, so she didn't have to sit down and actually study.

We do that a lot in life. Instead of actually taking the action needed, we get stuck in the planning and preparing phase. If you want to start a business or make a job out of a hobby, you will need to take the first step.

The first step is always going to be the hardest, but it is something you need to do. In all your planning, make sure you know what action you need to take and then do it. One of the best things you can do is set a deadline for yourself to take the first step. This makes it a commitment, and you are more likely to follow through.

STARTING YOUR OWN BUSINESS

Okay, so now we've gotten all of that out of the way, and you are looking to start up your own business. You don't have to wait until you are older to start a business. There are so many teenagers that have started businesses out of their homes, and this has set them up to be businesspeople when they are older. You can start a small business using a skill that you have already, so you know what it's like to handle money and run the operations of a business. You may not be doing this exact same thing when you graduate, but at least you have an idea of what it takes to run a business.

Write Down Your Ideas

The first thing you need to do is write down all your business ideas. You might be someone who has a ton of ideas. However, if you have way too many, it can be difficult to narrow it down. Having a list right in front of you will help you to weigh out the pros and cons so you can pick one to start with.

Think about what's going to be the easiest for you to start and what you think you will enjoy the most. Then you can choose that idea. If it doesn't work out, you can always go back to the list and pick another one.

Do Your Research

Once you have narrowed down your idea, it is time to start researching. See if there are any other businesses in your area that are doing something similar to you. Perhaps you want to start a dog walking business, then you would need to go online and find out if there aren't any dog walking businesses in your area. If there are none, this could either be a really good thing or a bad thing. Ask yourself why there are no dog-walking businesses in the area. Perhaps there aren't enough people who need someone to walk the dogs. If this is the case, then you are probably not going to be that successful. However, if there is a need but someone just hasn't started it up yet, then you might have hit a business gold mine.

Doing your research also helps you to understand your competition. It's not a bad thing to have competition, and you can actually learn from them. Look at how they market themselves on social media and on their websites. You can also look at the types of products and services they have so you can replicate this. It is usually easier to start a business when there is already a market for the product or service. Just make sure you can offer something slightly different that will make you stand out from the crowd.

Start Planning

Now, you will need to start planning. Your plan needs to include financial planning, as well as starting up the actual business. You might need some finances in order to get started, so you need to know how much. Think about how much you will need for marketing and for supplies. Try and be as realistic as possible with this. Once you know how much your product or service is going to cost you, you can then set the price you will be charging the customers. Make sure you are charging a competitive rate so you do not charge too little or way too much. You will also need to decide how long your product or service will take to make or develop. This way, when people order from you, you can give them an accurate waiting time.

Planning also includes looking at different suppliers so you can get the right prices. You will also need to do some research on your potential customers and see what they need. All of this should be written down on your business plan so you can easily find it. If you need to ask your parents or another adult for some money to help start up your business, you should know exactly how much you need and be able to tell them what your business is all about. This will make them a lot more likely to invest in your business.

Take Action

After all the planning is done, make sure you are willing to take action. Don't stay too long in the planning phase because then you might get stuck there. It is always best to take action as soon as possible so you can gain momentum.

IN REAL LIFE

Juliette was a 16-year-old girl, and she just wanted to hang out with other girls who were her age. She saw that there wasn't really a safe place online for girls around her age to just have fun and connect with each other. This is when she got the idea to start up a business called Miss O and Friends. She needed some help to finance the website since she was still in school and didn't really have any money. She asked her parents to help her out, and they were happy to fund the website.

She designed it and made sure that it was a good place for teen girls to connect with each other. The girls could talk about issues that were specific to the age group and get advice if they needed to. It is a great place to find new friends and to have some fun safely online. Her website launched in 2012 and just continued to grow. At one point, it had 10 million monthly visitors, which is absolutely crazy. The website and her business are valued at over $15 million. It's crazy to see how an idea can turn into a real business that benefits her and many other young girls.

Juliette decided she was not going to wait until she was older in order to make a difference and start a business. What was just an idea because she noticed there was a gap in the market became a multi-million dollar business. If you are willing to put in the work and try something new, then you could have a story similar to this. There are also many other ways you can make money. One of these ways is through real estate investing. We did touch on that a little bit in a previous chapter, but now we're going to dive in a bit deeper in the next chapter.

STRATEGY 4—BUILDING WEALTH THROUGH REAL ESTATE INVESTING

"90% of all millionaires become so through owning real estate."

— ANDREW CARNEGIE

Real estate is probably one of the most solid investment decisions anyone could make. However, as a teenager, you probably don't have enough money to invest in real estate right now. Don't worry, your time will come, and you will be able to invest in real estate at some point. In the meantime, it is a good idea to know what this type of investment looks like so you can be prepared for it. Since it is something that costs quite a bit of money, it is always a good idea to plan and prepare for it as early as possible. This way when you are older, you will be able to purchase a property and start investing as soon as possible.

REAL ESTATE INVESTING AND THE BENEFITS

Real estate investing is when you purchase a property, or you invest in a property indirectly. Essentially real estate is all about physical property. This is one of the best investments out there because the price of housing and property tend to continuously grow over time.

There are definitely some exceptions to the rule, but if you are able to do your research properly and purchase the right property, then you will set yourself up well.

The other great thing about investing in real estate is that you can do it in many different ways. You can make a passive income through real estate, or you can use it as a business. Even if you don't do anything with your property, you could likely make money from it. One of the most important things that you should consider is the location of the property. The location is what will determine the price at the end of the day. Some people only look at the physical property, but that is definitely a mistake. If you look at the price of property in a city, you'll see that it is usually a lot more expensive to live closer to the hustle and bustle than if you were to live on the outskirts. This is because the location in a city tends to be more in demand because it's easier to get around and there is a different lifestyle. There are even cases where you can get a house in one area and a one-bedroom apartment in another area for the same price. This is why research is key.

When you invest in real estate, you shouldn't expect the same returns as you would get if you invested in the stock market. The growth is definitely slower, but it is also more stable. The other thing that is important to understand about real estate is that it doesn't fluctuate the same way the stock market does. It is a lot steadier, and you will see a steady growth in your investment with very little chance of decline.

Another great thing about real estate is that you can leverage it. This is a fancy way of saying you can purchase an investment without actually using your own money. When you are buying a property, you will most likely need to get a loan or a mortgage in order to pay for it. You will need a sizable down payment, but depending on the type of property and your mortgage broker, you can get one as low as a 3% down payment. This means you only have to pay 3% of the total price of the property upfront. The rest of the money will be paid through the mortgage. If you want to rent out the property, then your tenants will be paying for the mortgage. You will charge the tenant a specific amount of money to stay in the property and can use that money to pay toward the mortgage. This means that you are not using any of your own money for the investment but will benefit from having a solid investment and a property. There are also some tax benefits to owning a property which is also a huge plus.

When the mortgage is completely paid off, you now have a property that you can use as a form of passive income. Some people decide to rent out their property long-term, which means the tenants will be living there for years on end. If someone is living in your property for multiple years, you'll be getting paid for that, and you really don't have to do anything. You will be a landlord, so you will need to take care of the property within reason. However, most long-term tenants will handle things on their own. You just need to make sure you have a solid contract in place so everyone knows what their responsibilities are when it comes to the property.

THE DIFFERENT TYPES

Understanding the different types of property and real estate investments you can make is essential. Not everything is going to work for every person. You don't want to get caught up in an investment that is unsustainable for you and that is simply not going to work. When it comes to real estate, it's always important that you do your research as much as possible. Since this is quite a big investment, you can't just wing it.

REIT

A real estate investment trust is a great way to start investing in property without having to actually buy a property. It is quite similar to a mutual fund since many investors will pool all the money together, and this money will be used to invest in real estate. This means you can get involved in real estate investing at a much lower price, but your return on the investment will probably be smaller. The other benefit of doing this is that you don't actually have to take care of or manage a property which can be a lot of work.

Crowdfunding

Another way to invest in property without actually owning the property is through crowdfunding platforms. These can work similarly to REITs. The difference is that these are not bought and sold on the stock exchange markets. Essentially a property will be put up on the platform, and anyone who is willing to invest will invest a certain amount of money. This will allow an individual to purchase the property, and the profits through rental income or any other kind of property activity will be shared amongst everyone who invested.

Residential Real Estate

Residential real estate just means that it is a property where people live. Your house or apartment is a residential property. An investor can make money through residential property by buying it and renting it out to tenants or house flipping. House flipping is when someone purchases a property, usually at a lower price, and then renovates it to sell it at a higher price. This type of real estate investment makes money quite quickly, but it is essential to do your research prior since you need to make sure people will be willing to buy a property in that area for the price you are looking to sell it for. You can also make money through residential real estate by simply buying the property and waiting a few years to sell it for a profit. If you live in a house or an apartment, this is typically what people do.

Commercial Real Estate

Property that is used by businesses is called commercial real estate. This can be anything from an office building to a mall. The owner of commercial real estate will rent out rooms, areas, or the entire building to a business, and this is how they would make money. Other examples of commercial real estate are warehouses, restaurants, or factories. These are quite expensive to start investing in since the properties are much larger, but the profit is also larger because business owners will pay more for rent. Businesses also tend to stay much longer, so it is a steady form of income.

Land

It is also possible to buy raw land that doesn't have anything built on it. This isn't a good investment opportunity for a beginner because there is a ton of research that needs to go into it to make sure the land is good to build on and the location is something that will possibly be in demand in the future. An investor looking to invest in land needs to know the ins and outs of the regulations and building codes as well as the environmental impact that will go into building. This can get very technical, so if it is your first investment, it is probably not a good idea to dip your toe into raw land. This might be a future goal when you are more solid in your knowledge of real estate investment.

A FEW TIPS AND TRICKS

There are a few small things you can do when it comes to real estate investing that will make a huge difference. If you do these things, you will be able to make smarter decisions when it comes to real estate, and you will probably be able to make a lot more profit.

Look Into Location

One of the most important things you can look out for when you are investing in real estate is the location. This is actually more important than the actual property you are buying. You will need to understand the location you are purchasing a property so that you can be sure it is a good buy.

But what makes a good location? It is going to take a lot of research to be sure that the neighborhood you want to purchase in will be profitable. Firstly, you will need to look at what is available in that neighborhood. A neighborhood that has a high population density, which means there are lots of people living in the area, is a good place to start. Areas that are quite desolate and don't have a lot of people typically won't have high property values. Another thing to look out for is whether or not the neighborhood is developing. If there is new construction taking place in and around town, you know there are people investing in it. Look out for amenities such as shopping centers, hospitals, and other things that will take care of people's needs.

The next thing you can look into are things such as the crime rate. Areas with a high crime rate will be cheaper because it is more dangerous to live there. Easy access to public transportation and being able to walk around easily and safely are also good things to keep an eye out for. A family-friendly area that has good school options as well as parks and other leisure activities also increase the price of a property in the area.

Buy at Low Prices

There are going to be times when property is priced lower than normal. When you are buying property for profit and not just to live in, it is important to look out for these moments. There are many reasons property might be selling for less. This includes when the economy is taking a dip. Times like these lead people to sell their properties because they want to downsize. For example, in a recession, people naturally have less money. They might not be able to afford a larger house, so they decide they want to sell it for something cheaper. Since they know they are in a recession and they want to sell their property quickly, they will put the house up for sale at a cheaper rate. You can end up saving a ton of money by looking for opportunities like this. The lower you are able to buy, the more profit you will make from your property.

Know All the Costs

The price of a property is not just the amount you will be paying when you first buy it. There are lots of other costs that come into play. A property needs to be maintained, and this costs money. You will need to consider paying things like utilities and property tax. Utilities include things like electricity, trash, pick up, and water. If your property is part of a homeowners association, you would need to pay a fee to them as well. A homeowners association takes care of things in the neighborhood and makes sure the neighborhood runs smoothly, and everybody is playing their part.

Increase the Value

There are tons of things you can do to increase the value of your property without spending a whole bunch of money. Many people make the mistake of selling it as is, and then they miss out on a large chunk of profit. For example, simply giving the house a fresh coat of paint can do wonders for it. It will look brand new, and you can probably sell it or rent it out for more because of this.

It is always a good idea to be on the lookout for what people want in a place to stay. This will help you to add value to your property easily. Perhaps you could add a cleaning service or even a security guard or concierge to your property. This works if you have multiple properties. You could always charge a little bit more on your rental fees because you're adding value through these services. It makes your property look a lot more attractive, and people are willing to pay more for these small conveniences.

Understand the Rules

Every area, country, and state has its own rules and regulations in place when it comes to real estate. If you are not aware of them, then you could be at risk of making a huge mistake down the line. Rather than putting yourself in this horrible situation, you should do your research to make sure you are aware of all the rules and regulations in your area.

Be aware of things like zoning laws because this can stop you from building an additional room on your property or a second-story floor. You might think it's a good idea to place vending machines around your property or even provide meals to your guests or tenants. However, there are some places that prohibit food services or are very strict when it comes to this. You could end up getting sued or taken to court because you didn't follow the food service rules. You might be allowed to do these things if you get a permit, but there is work and costs involved with getting a permit. Understand all of these little facts before you get started in renovating or adding value to your property.

Quick Facts

REITs can help you get involved with real estate with very little money. It is a great first step!	Leveraging real estate means buying real estate with someone else's money. You can do this by renting out a bought property and using the rent to pay off the mortgage.
You can find the type of real estate investing that works for you at different stages of your life.	Small things can increase the value of a house by a large amount.
Always think of location first.	The rules and laws surrounding property are different based on area and location. Always do your research before buying.

STRATEGY 5—DEVELOPING A POSITIVE MONEY MINDSET

"Most wealth is inconspicuous. The man down the street driving the nice car and living in the mansion could easily have greater debt and a lower net worth than the stealthy and wealthy plumber who drives a beat-up truck but seems to work only when he doesn't feel like fishing."

— LORAL LANGEMEIER

THE IMPORTANCE OF THE MONEY MINDSET

Mindset is one of the most important things when it comes to money. This may sound really strange because it seems like actual money should be the most important thing when it comes to… well, money. The thing with money is that it is just a tool that we use to get what we really want. If money did not buy anything, then we would not care about it. It would just be random pieces of paper with old guys' faces on it!

Let's look at it this way. Do you have a dad or uncle who has a toolbox or tool shed? There are probably hammers, scissors, nails, screwdrivers, and a few more things in there. Do you think those adults would still have those things if these things didn't serve a purpose or if they didn't help them with stuff around the house? Probably not. Even the coolest tool would have no value if it wasn't useful. People like to have these tools because they need them for the end goal. It is important for someone to hang up a photo frame with precious memories in it. In order to do that, they need a hammer and nails. It is important to install a bookshelf for your favorite books, so you would need a drill, screws, and a screwdriver. The importance of the tool is in how you use it and not in the tool itself.

When you start looking at money in this way, you don't have to be so obsessed with getting more money because it is not the most important thing. The important thing is what the money can do for you and how you can use it in your life. This is a healthier way to look at money. This is a good start for a money mindset, but it is not the end. You also have to think of things positively and abundantly. This means throwing out any belief that is limiting you. If you get hung up on money and don't believe there is anything you can do to increase your wealth, then that is what is going to be true for you. People usually follow in the footsteps of their thoughts. The more positive you are, the more opportunities you will find in your life.

When you feel like what you have will never be enough, it leads to some bad money habits. You might want to hoard all your money and never spend it because you are scared to waste it. Or you might go to the other end of the spectrum where you spend all your money when you get it because you just want to enjoy it while you can. Both are bad ways to handle money, and there needs to be a better balance.

Don't Let the Myths Get To You

When there are negative money mindsets; there are also myths that pop up. These are things that can really hold you back. If you are able to identify the myth, then you can avoid it. The first and biggest myth that surrounds money is that you are simply not enough unless you have enough. Money can quickly become an identity, and people can only see their worth based on how much they have in the bank. This actually plays on something called a scarcity mindset, where you think you don't have enough and you urgently need to take action to make it. This leads to making so many bad decisions because you don't allow yourself the time to think about it, and you can actually get caught up in scams that promote getting rich quickly.

The next myth is, "Everything is exactly how it seems." Now that we live in a social media world, it can be easy to get distracted by what is happening online. We see people living the good life. Just because these people look like they're living the dream and appear wealthy does not mean they are. There isn't a lot of transparency when it comes to social media, so you could be comparing yourself to something that is completely false or unrealistic. Don't get in the habit of envying what other people have.

Another big myth that surrounds money is that things can change in a matter of weeks or months. Everybody wants their life to change with the snap of a finger, but the truth is this hardly ever happens. If you want your money and your finances to change, it's going to take planning and time in order to start seeing results. If anyone tells you that you can make a whole lot of money in a few weeks, then they are probably lying to you. Look, I'm not saying that it's impossible to make large amounts of money in a short amount of time, but this is highly unlikely. It is better to live with realistic standards, so you don't feel like you've been cheated if it doesn't work out the way you thought.

DON'T LET YOUR MONEY BELIEFS LIMIT YOU

What you believe about money can come from so many different places. Some people see how their parents or other adults in their life handle the money, and this filters down to them. Someone who has parents who are very frugal and don't spend money will probably be similar to that. However, this is not always the case because it can go in the opposite direction. If your parents are very strict with money and don't spend it on any luxuries, you might feel like you want a different life when you're older. This might cause you to overspend and just buy luxuries without thinking about it. It is important to understand where your beliefs about money come from so you can get to the root of the problem if there's one.

With a little bit of planning and thinking about things clearly, you can change the way you think about money.

If you start framing things in a more positive light, you'll see more opportunities, and it will be easier to look at money from a healthier perspective. For example, a lot of people believe that the only way they can make a lot of money and be financially secure is to get a corporate desk job. This could definitely be true for some people, but it is not the overarching rule. Having this kind of mindset can stop you from pursuing your dreams and maybe even stop you from starting your own business.

At the end of the day, your money mindset should be flexible. There are tons of ways you can make money and reach your dreams. If you're able to look at things realistically but also positively, that is going to be key. You are able to do something you love and make money if you have a plan in place for it. People do it all the time. You just need to know how. I would go so far as to say that people who love what they do tend to make more money because they don't have to force themselves to do something they do not like.

Another huge mindset problem I've seen recently is that people believe that money is evil. Money is not evil, and it's not good either. It is just a neutral thing. It is how you use it and how you think about it that makes it either good or bad. Thinking that money is something bad or evil can lead you to completely avoid it.

And while money can't actually buy happiness, it can bring happiness into your life. You are able to use money for good and for things that will improve your life. Money might not be the be all and end all but it definitely has some value. If you grew up believing that money is the root of all evil and look down on people who do have money, it is a good idea to start changing this belief. This is something that's really going to limit you as you grow up because it's training you to run away from money instead of training you how to use money for your own benefit.

Another limiting mindset is that where you are is where you will always be. If you grew up in a family that isn't rich or you don't have a lot of money to start off with, it can be so easy to believe that this is just how your life played out. Some of the richest people in life are ones that are self-made. This means that they didn't need their parents' money in order to become wealthy and increase their standard of living. They decided to do it on their own, and you can too. You don't necessarily need money in order to make more money. If you have an idea and are willing to put in the work, then you can go very far. Where you are now, it's just the starting point, and as you take steps in order to build wealth and become a more successful person, you will see the money rolling in afterward.

Every person deserves to have enough money to live the life that they want. The good news is that this is possible for all of us. If you remember that money is just a tool, you will look for ways to use it in a way that's going to be beneficial for you. It's not something that's scary; it's not something that's going to hold you back or make you into an evil person. Money is just a thing, and you can choose how you want to use it.

CREATING A POSITIVE MINDSET ABOUT MONEY

Now that we have talked about a negative money mindset and what it can do, we also want to dive into creating a more positive money mindset. This is so important, and it's something that you are probably going to need to do throughout your life. Negative mindsets and thoughts can always creep in, so it is important to check yourself every now and then.

Move Forward From the Past

At this point in your life, you might not have made too many financial mistakes, but as you grow up, you'll probably make at least a few. Mistakes are how we learn, and in most cases, it is pretty much inevitable. We end up doing things based on emotion or because we got some bad information. Even if you have made a few bad choices with your money, it is time to forgive yourself. If you are resentful about the decisions you have made in the past, it's going to make it very difficult to trust yourself to make better choices in the future. Rather than being mad about the mistakes you've made, be thankful that you have learned from them. Now you are a better person and can avoid those mistakes in the future.

Have a Plan

Having a plan for your money is essential to being able to use it effectively. We usually call this plan financial goals and a budget. You first set your financial goals so you know what is important to you, and then you work it into your budget so you have a step-by-step plan to get there. This will help you to see yourself progressing, so even if you aren't reaching your goals as fast as you would like, you can see that there is progress happening. Simply moving toward a goal can make you a lot happier, and you'll feel a lot more secure in your finances.

Make Room In Your Budget For Enjoyment

It is all well and good to have a budget that is filled with important life goals, but you also have to have some enjoyment in your life too. A lot of financial gurus tell people they have to cut out everything unnecessary from their life so they can save for things that are important to them. It is important to think about your financial goals and what is important to you, but it's also important for you to be happy right now. If you are only thinking about the future, then you are going to have a miserable time in the present. You will never be able to go back and live this day again, so you need to make sure that you are balancing your future and your present.

There are some things in your life that other people might think are unnecessary but that actually bring enjoyment to you. For some people having a gym membership is not worth it because they don't use it and prefer to take a jog outside. However, you might be the type of person that loves going to the gym, and it really adds something to your life. Even though you have to pay for a gym membership, if it makes you happy, then do it. This is something important to you, and it is benefiting you as well. Maybe you are someone who really enjoys going out to a fancy dinner every once in a while. Sure, cooking at home definitely will save you some money, but it's probably not going to fulfill you in the same way. Instead of cutting out the fancy dinners completely, you can commit to doing it once a month and set a specific budget for how much you are willing to spend. This way, you have the thing that you enjoy doing, and you don't have to cut it out completely. This will actually make it a lot easier to reach other financial goals because you're not going to feel like you're always in some sort of lack.

Always Be Thankful

Gratitude is one of the most important things that we can all implement in our life. I remember social media went through a huge moment when everybody was talking about gratitude and writing gratitude journals. This is when people would write out things they are grateful for every morning and evening. It seems like this practice has fallen out of popularity, but it doesn't mean that it isn't something good to follow. There are tons of benefits to practicing gratitude.

When you are grateful for the things you have now, you don't feel like you have to keep getting more or have to pretend. At the end of the day, where you are now is based on the decisions you made in the past. While you might've made some mistakes, you have also grown and become a better person. Being grateful for the things you have now allows you to look at your life from a more positive perspective. You won't feel like you always need the next best thing because you know that your life is already amazing.

If you struggle with staying grateful, why not pick up the habit of a gratitude journal? It's usually better to do this in the morning because you can set your mind to gratitude from the beginning of the day. All you have to do is write out two or three things that you are grateful for that day. You will quickly realize that there are a lot more positive things in your life than you might have thought.

TAKE IT STEP BY STEP

Now is the time when you can create a plan for yourself to create a more positive money mindset. Below is a checklist of things that you can do. However, you can feel free to change it up however you want, based on your own personality and needs.

- Identify any money myths you have believed.
- Think about how your parents view money and how that has impacted you.
- Write out a counter statement for all the myths and beliefs you had in the past. Make sure it is positive.
- Forgive any money mistakes you have made in the past.
- Track your financial goals so you can see how far you have come.
- Allow yourself to enjoy your money every now and then.
- Be grateful for where you are and what you have.

7

STRATEGY 6—NAVIGATING FINANCIAL CHALLENGES AND PITFALLS

When I was younger, there was this video game where the character was in a jungle. The goal was to get to the finish line by avoiding pitfalls or holes in the ground. There were also some jungle animals that used to chase you, so you had to be quick. The first few levels were pretty easy, as you just had to jump over the holes that were clearly visible. As you got onto the harder levels, you had to be a lot quicker, and the holes were larger. Not only that but some of them were hidden. This meant that I could never finish the higher levels in one go. I had to keep starting back from certain checkpoints and trying again. After some planning and practice, I would move on to the next level until I eventually won the game.

This is actually pretty similar to the pitfalls we have when it comes to money. Some of the traps or holes that we can fall into are very easily avoidable. We can see them from a distance because they are so small. It's easier for us to hop over them and completely avoid them. Then there are others that are much bigger and well hidden. It makes it a lot harder for us to avoid these things, and sometimes we get caught. Even if we have the best financial plan set out in front of us, we can still make a few mistakes. This might sound very discouraging, but the truth is that mistakes help us to learn. It is a good idea to avoid as many mistakes and pitfalls as possible, but if you do land up in one, it's okay. Just make sure you have a plan to move forward, and that you have taken the time to learn from this mistake.

In this chapter, we are going to go through a few financial mistakes that teenagers typically make. We will also talk about how you can avoid them if possible. This is going to set you up for your future and allow you to be in a good financial position when you are managing your own money and handling your own finances.

TEENAGE FINANCIAL CHALLENGES

As a teenager, you probably have a lot of adults in your life thinking that you don't have any financial challenges. Anyone of any age can have a financial struggle or financial challenge that they have to overcome. This is very normal, and even though it might not be as stressful as what an adult would go through, this is still your story and your challenge. Understanding what challenges you go through financially can actually help you when you are an adult. You'll be able to deal with your financial problems a lot better because you've learned how to deal with smaller issues already.

Never Having Enough Money!

Ugh, feeling like you never have enough money is the worst! There might be tons of things that you want to buy, but you just don't have enough money. This can make you feel like you are an outsider because everyone else around you is going to all these fancy places and buying all these cool things. It can make you feel like you are just not in with the popular crowd or that you are worth less than them. Let's add social media into it, and this can make it even worse.

It is important to realize that just because other people have more money and they are able to do more doesn't mean that you are less than them. Let me tell you something about life. There are going to be points in life when people have more money and others when they have less. There is probably going to be a point in your life when you have more money or more opportunities than the people you are looking at right now.

Spending More Than You Have

When you are a teenager, it is so easy to spend more money than what you are actually making. This is because you can always go to your parents and many parents are willing to give you a little extra if you need it. This can be a really bad habit because you are teaching yourself not to follow a budget or plan. Instead, whenever you need something, you are getting money from somewhere else, and when you are older, it's not going to be your parents. This is teaching you how to be in debt. If you notice you are doing this, it is time to create a budget and only spend the amount that you are actually making.

Trying To Keep Up With Friends

Have you ever watched the TV show *Keeping Up With the Kardashians*? It is an incredibly popular show, and most people have heard about this family. The reason the show has this name is that the Kardashians are incredibly wealthy, and they live the lifestyle that many people want to live. They have tons of houses and are always going on these expensive vacations and wearing the most expensive clothes. It makes people want to live the exact same lifestyle or aspire to it at some point in their life.

We can also do this when it comes to our friends and the people that are around us. We can look at all the things they have in the types of lifestyles they are living and want that as well. This makes us compare our lives to the lives of other people, and then we are unhappy. The thing is that most of these things are just trends. You can ask your parents or any other adults, and they will tell you the things that they used to do and, like when they were younger, they don't really do or have anymore. As the trends change, so do they. It's just something temporary, so trying to live your life up to a certain standard isn't really beneficial to you. If you want to buy all the coolest clothes and technology in a few months or years, it's not going to mean anything. This means there's no point in trying to compare yourself now to what your friends have or what they are doing. It's not really going to have any long-term benefit for you, and you'll be a lot happier if you just lived your life within your means now.

Not Wanting to Work

Learning the value of money is incredibly important when you are younger. If you don't work for your money, it can be easy to think that money really does grow on trees. You won't be motivated to budget properly and create financial goals if there is no value being placed on money. If you can quickly run to your parents and get money whenever you want, you aren't really learning how to manage it properly.

This isn't completely your fault, but you do have the power to change it. If you have an honest conversation with your parents and let them know that you want to learn how to be more responsible with money, they might be willing to change the way they handle money with you. This might be a big change for you, but it's definitely going to help you in the long run. Let them know that you want to learn how to budget and manage your money properly and that you want to know the value of what you get. Some parents love to spoil their children, and it comes from a good place. This is definitely not a bad thing but work with your parents so you can be set up for success when you are ready to handle your own finances. This means setting boundaries on how much your parents give you and when they give you money.

Other People Always Paying For You or Vice Versa

Peer pressure is a normal thing that most teenagers go through. If you are around the age of 14 or 15, this is when it peaks. By the time you are a little bit older, usually after high school, you won't feel it as bad. However, during this peer pressure stage of your life, money can cause problems for you. If you look at the things that your friends have, you might also want those things. Your friends might be going out all the time, and you also want to join them. If you don't have the money, then your friends might offer to pay for you all the time. Or perhaps you have some friends that don't have money, and you are the one paying for them all the time.

If this happens once in a while, it might not be a big deal, but if it's a pattern, then it's something you need to watch out for. Being on the receiving end of this can lead you down a debt or credit cycle when you are older. You are not learning how to use your own money, and even though other people are being generous toward you, it's difficult for you to learn financial responsibility this way. On the other hand, you might be the one with a lot of money and want to pay for other people. This is definitely fine once in a while, but if you are always doing it, then you become the provider for these other people. It's easy for people to take advantage of those who are generous. This is why it is important to manage your money properly so that you are not taken advantage of in any way.

Parents' Money Problems

It is so common for teenagers to be worried about their parents' financial situations. If your parents aren't the wealthiest, you can start getting nervous about whether or not you can afford certain things. You might notice that your parents are being a little more frugal with how they spend their money, or that they aren't buying the types of things they used to. In this case, it is always a good idea to have an honest conversation with your parents.

Parents don't like to burden their children with financial issues, and that might be the case here. Even though your parents are trying to protect you, if you are feeling stressed out by the financial changes that are happening, then it's not doing you any good. Showing your parents that you are old enough and mature enough to understand finances and what they are going through is going to help them be more honest with you. This will also help you to navigate the financial situation a bit better. You will be a lot more understanding if your parents cannot afford certain things, and you might look for ways to save and make more money to help out. This helps you to be a lot more responsible, and it might also take a bit of pressure off your parents.

CREDIT AND DEBT

As you get closer to the point in life where you are going to be more financially independent, it is important to understand credit and debt. Now we have touched briefly on these two topics, but it is important to dive slightly deeper, so you have a better understanding of what it is. Sometimes people think they have to avoid these two things completely. Otherwise, their finances are going to be ruined. However, this is not actually the case. Just like money, these two things can be tools and can be used in a positive way. Most people just don't know how to use it and end up getting themselves into trouble.

Let's first talk about how credit actually works. When we talk about credit, it's not just about your credit card. If you think about the word credit, it is used in many other contexts. Like when we say, give credit where credit is due. This saying means that we need to acknowledge the good that someone else has done. A credit statement or credit report can do the same thing. It shows lenders that you are able to take out a loan or borrow money and are good for it. When people look at your credit report, they are looking to see whether or not you are responsible with your money and can handle borrowing more.

Debt and credit are different because the definitions and what they can do for you are not the same. Credit gives you the ability to purchase something you don't have the money for right now. You can think of this as future purchasing power. You can choose whether you are going to use it or not. When you have a credit card, you will be given a specific limit on the credit card, and it's up to you to decide whether you want to use it or just leave it as is. If you do use your credit card, then it will form part of the debt. Debt is when you owe someone money. You would have agreed to pay back a certain amount at a certain interest rate and will need to make sure you are in good standing. Otherwise, this can impact your credit score and other aspects of your finances.

In life, you're probably not going to be able to afford everything in cash. If you plan on purchasing a property or another large investment or item, you might need to take out a loan or use a credit card. In order to do this, you need to receive a loan from someone who trusts that you can pay it back. This is why having a good credit score is so important. There are lots of things that are used to create a credit report. In order to check out your credit score, you will need to have an account that offers credit. This will need to be up and running for around six months, and then your credit score will be calculated. This is also known as the FICO score. You will get a number between 300 and 850. There are some calculators at work that are slightly different, but this is the standard. The higher your credit score, the better for you. It means that you will be more likely to be offered financial assistance, loans, and higher credit.

It is so important to start building your credit as young as possible so there are no hiccups when you are older and want to purchase something. Your credit score is worked out in terms of how well you've handled your debt, the types of debt you have, the length of time you've had it, and how long you have been building your credit. You might be wondering how you can start building your credit at such a young age because you don't have access to a credit card. This confuses many teenagers, and I totally understand that. The good news is there are things you can do to help build your credit even at a younger age. One of these things is to be added as an authorized user on an adult's credit card. Your parents can do this for you, so make sure to have an open and honest conversation with them. When you choose someone, make sure that this person has good credit; otherwise, it could affect you negatively.

AVOID THE PITFALLS

While there are definitely situations where you will need to use credit or take out a loan, this shouldn't be all the time. If you decide to use your credit card and spend all over the place, then you'll end up in a financial pitfall. Most people don't even see it coming, and that's how they land up in a big problem. Debt can creep up on you, so it is important to make sure you're making good financial decisions as often as possible.

Know Your Due Dates

When you get older, you'll have to pay bills. These are what you owe specific companies because you are using their services. For example, you might have to pay for Wi-Fi or a cell phone contract. Your rent, electricity, other utilities, contracts, and subscriptions will all fall under this. Most of them will have a specific due date, and you will need to pay it before or on the due date. If you miss the due date, then your service will be suspended until you are able to pay. This could also impact your credit score because now you are in debt.

To avoid this, you need to know exactly when your due dates are and make it obvious. Putting it on your calendar app on your phone is very helpful. When the due date is closing in, you will get a reminder, and you can make payment. Another great option is to call all your service providers and ask if you can change the due date to a specific one. You can choose the day after you get paid so you can pay all of your bills at one time. This will make it a lot easier for you. Another option is to set up automatic payments so the money goes out of your account without you having to do anything. You just have to make sure there is enough money in your bank account for the automatic payment to clear.

Have Your Credit in Your Budget

We've already discussed how it is important to use credit but you do have to use it wisely. This means it's always best to plan for using your credit. The main goal for your month-to-month spending should be to use credit only to build up your credit score. You should not be using it to actually purchase unnecessary items. Remember, when we were talking about budgeting, you have to only spend the amount of money you make.

A good way to use credit is to have a look at your monthly spending. You'll probably have a specific amount allocated to things like your groceries or your gas. You can use your credit card to pay for these things and set aside that amount in your budget. At the end of the month, you will pay back the money you spent, so you do not have to go into debt. This way, you are still using your credit card, but you aren't putting yourself in a bad financial position.

When you do have a credit card, it is so easy to just swipe when you want something. It doesn't have any repercussions right now, so it's easy to just not think about it. However, you can get yourself into a huge amount of financial stress if you do not keep track of your credit card and spending. If you know that you cannot control your spending when it comes to your credit card, it might be best to just leave it at home. This way you can just use your debit card for your regular spending and you know there's going to be a limit to it. You can take your credit card out when you want to purchase something specific.

Save First

Saving for the things you want is so important. Instead of quickly swiping and putting things on your credit card, take some time to save for the item. This can be easily put into your budget so you can prioritize it. This will also allow you time to think about whether you actually want the item or not. Sometimes we can impulse buy items that look cool, but we don't actually need them.

Avoid Overextending Yourself

If you can't do something or can't afford something; it is totally fine to say so. Speak up and let your friends and family know that whatever is happening is something that you cannot afford. I know it can be so difficult to say no to people, especially when you actually want to do that thing or spend your money. It's just not going to be good for your finances right now.

Learning how to say no to other people is very important when you are working on your financial health. If you have already spent your entertainment budget for the month and your friends say they want to go watch a movie, you know that you don't have the money for it. Sometimes it's not a case of saying absolutely no. You can make another suggestion. Suggest doing something cheaper so that you can afford to hang out with your friends or you can ask if they can move the movie date to the next month. This way you are still able to do things but you are working within your budget.

WHOOPS, I MESSED UP! NOW WHAT?

Even somebody who is amazing at managing their finances will probably make a mistake once or twice. Unfortunately, this is just something that we all get ourselves into, but the first step is always acknowledging that there was a mistake made. If you are aware that you overspent or you got yourself into debt that you didn't mean to, then at least you can start working on a plan. If you're in denial, it's going to be very difficult to get out of the mistake, and you'll probably end up worse off.

Once you know that you have made a mistake, it's time to assess the damage. This is going to look different, depending on the type of mistake you made. If it is overspending on your credit card, then have a look at how much you owe in total. At this point, you can feel very disheartened but don't allow yourself to get too stressed out about it. Almost any situation can be fixed if you have the right plan. Accept the situation that you are in for now, and then start looking at different options to get out of the problem.

In the example of overspending on your credit card, you can start thinking about paying it back. You will need to pay back more than what you would regularly pay back so you can finish paying off the debt completely. This means that you will have to look at your budget and see where you can cut back so you can put more money into paying off the credit card. Depending on how much you spend, this could be a long-term thing or something that can be fixed in a few months.

Regardless of the type of mistake you have made, it is so important to make clear goals for yourself. Know exactly how much money you need to put into your goals every month and put measures in place so you can actually reach them. This will help you to prioritize the things that are most important so you can recover as soon as possible.

In some cases, you might not be able to do it on your own, and you might need to talk to somebody about it. It is usually best to talk to somebody who is good with their finances or maybe you need to get in touch with a professional. This way, you can find a solution quicker, and you will have someone to be accountable to. In some cases, you might have to completely freeze your spending and stop buying things that are unnecessary. Certain mistakes take drastic measures, like saying no to something you really want but is not a necessity. Remember to add everything to your budget so you can look at your finances from a broader perspective.

It's also important to understand that not all mistakes can be fixed in a matter of weeks. Sometimes you will have to spend a few months or even years working on it. That is okay as long as you are tracking your progress; you will eventually get there. Thinking that you can solve the problem as soon as possible can actually leave you feeling very disheartened if you can't. This is why it's important to be as realistic as you can when it comes to your finances.

IN REAL LIFE

After Cory had graduated from college, he started working at a good and stable company. He enjoyed his job, but he wasn't really earning as much as he would've liked. His friends were always going to fun events and living a lifestyle that he also wanted. This is what prompted him to take out a credit card. When he first got the credit card, he didn't want to use it all the time. It was just for emergencies and the occasional nice thing. He thought that it should be okay because, in a few years, he would get a promotion and earn more money, so he could pay it back if he owed something on the credit card.

Five years down the line and he ended up in tons of debt. In fact, he had to pay back $50,000 worth of debt, and it kept growing. Over the years, it wasn't just his credit card that he was using, but he was taking out loans for other items. He had started living a lifestyle that he couldn't afford, and he just kept spiraling down the rabbit hole. It's not where he wanted to be, but that's where his choices left him.

Unfortunately, he did not earn as much as he thought he would at this point in his life. There were some economic issues that caused the company not to give the increases they would've liked. This meant that Cory's plan to pay it off when he was earning more money was not working out for him. At this point, he felt his debt was so much that he simply could not get out of it. He knew that he needed some professional help, so he contacted a debt counselor. Honestly, she was a godsend because she went through everything to help develop a plan for him to pay off the debt. Sure, Cory had to pay a fee for her services, but it was well worth it because now he had a plan. She advised him that whenever he had a little extra money, it should always go toward paying off the debt, even if it was just $20 or $50. Every small amount counts. Since she was keeping him accountable, it was a huge motivation for him to keep going and just stay on track.

Over the next four years, he was able to pay off the debt completely. Once the credit card was paid off, he decided that he was going to cancel his credit card for the time being. He wanted a completely fresh start and didn't want to be tempted to get back into this situation again. He learned how to create a budget and prioritize his savings and spending goals. Managing his money was a lot easier now, and he wanted to see if you could do it without a credit card. After about a year, he decided he was going to get another credit card, but he was going to be a lot more responsible with it. He left it at home every time he went out and didn't use it for online purchases. This way, he was able to control his spending, and ever since then, he did not get into large amounts of debt again. He was able to learn his lesson and make better financial decisions for his future.

Cory needed some extra help to develop some good financial habits. These financial habits helped him get out of debt and stay out of debt. There are tons of financial habits that someone can have, and it is important to develop them as soon as possible. In the next chapter, we are diving into the money habits that will allow you to build success in your life for the long term.

STRATEGY 7—DEVELOPING EFFECTIVE MONEY HABITS FOR LONG-TERM SUCCESS

"It is tempting to try to get rich quickly, but the process of getting rich slowly and steadily via saving and long-term investing is tested and reliable."

— NIMI AKINKUGBE

We live in a world where everything can happen at the snap of a finger. We all want things to happen super quickly, so we can get the benefits of it now. It's not surprising that we are always looking for quick fixes since that is what we are basically trained to do. These days all you have to do is click a few buttons, and you can get your groceries, clothes, technology, or basically anything else delivered to your door the next day. You don't even have to leave your house to get a delicious meal from your favorite restaurant. Since everything is so easy and we live in this world where we get what we want when we want it, it can be very difficult to move out of that mindset.

The truth is that most good and sustainable things do take time. You won't be able to build a successful business in a matter of weeks. You can't get a degree in a few days. You definitely can't build sustainable wealth in a short time. All of these things take years to put into place and to grow. This means that you need to have good habits to help you. Habits are things that you do every day that lead you to success. These are small things that can change your entire life. The great thing about habits is that once you have put them in place, you will do them without thinking about them. It's like how most people just brush their teeth in the morning; It becomes a habit. This is a good habit, and it's probably the reason why your teeth are not rotting and falling out (thanks Mom and Dad!). You probably have quite a few good habits that you haven't even thought of. Imagine what habits could do if you were intentional in developing the right ones.

DEVELOPING HABITS THAT STICK

If you are struggling with setting up habits for your life, then the section is really going to help you. The advice here is not just for financial habits but can be applied to every other habit in your life. It will help you make habits that stick for the long term so you can make better choices and live a much more successful life.

Start With a Routine

A routine and a habit are two different things, but creating a routine can help you create a habit. A routine is a collection of small things that you do repeatedly. Then a habit can be birthed out of this. Sometimes we need something to trigger our brains into performing a habit, and that's why a routine works. So, if you want to build the habit of sitting down and creating a budget each month, you will need to think of a routine that will work with this.

The first place you can look is at what you are already doing. Look at your schedule and see how you can fit budgeting into it. Let's say on a Sunday, you do a full self-care Sunday routine. This is where you take care of your mental and physical health. You might do a skin-care routine and get your week sorted out. This is the perfect time to slip into budgeting. You can say that after you are done with your skincare and have tidied up your room, you will sit down and budget. Since you already have an established routine, it's easy to just add something to it. Eventually, budgeting will just form part of the routine, and it will be an easy habit to continue with.

Once you have built the habit, you might not need the routine to continue doing it. It's something that you are already used to doing, so if you have to move it to a different time or place in your week or your month, it will still work for you.

Know What You Are Doing

When you are trying to create a habit, you need to know exactly what that habit is. You won't be able to create a habit if you are too vague about how or what it actually is. For example, you can't say you want to be better with money and expect a habit to come from that. Dig a little deeper and specifically tell yourself what habit you are trying to build. Being better with money could be learning how to budget, tracking your spending, saving a certain amount each month, or writing down financial goals.

Expect a Few Setbacks

Even the most perfect person is going to have a little trouble when it comes to setting and sticking to habits. If it truly was easy, then everybody would have these awesome habits already instilled in them, but this is not the case. Because good habits are naturally more difficult to build than the bad ones, you are probably going to hit a few setbacks.

One of the biggest misconceptions is that you have to do something for 21 days in order for a habit to stick. This seems like a great guideline, but when people fail to keep the habit up for 21 days, they think they have to start all the way from the beginning. This becomes incredibly demotivating, and then they don't want to do it anymore. The truth is that a habit can take shorter or longer than 21 days to stick. It depends on the individual person and the type of habit you are trying to make work for you.

If you miss one or two days of your habit, it's not going to be the end of the world. You can just pick up where you left off and continue. Consistency is not about perfection. It's about trying to do your best over and over again.

Notice What Is Stopping You

We all have certain things in our life that block us from doing our best. If you keep failing at setting up your habits, it might be because you have one of these blockers in your life. It is a good idea to stop and think about what is actually causing you to fail. Perhaps you have set a savings goal for yourself for the month, but each month, you never have enough money to save. This means it's very difficult for you to set this habit as something concrete in your life.

Instead of just giving up and thinking that it's too difficult to implement this habit, you can take a step back and look at what is stopping you. When you set your budget at the beginning of the month, it may look like you have enough money to save, but when you want to put the money away, you realize you don't. This is very strange, so you decide that you are going to start tracking your spending to see where your money is going. It turns out that you end up spending some money on random items at the mall when you go out with your friends. This means that your money is not going toward saving because it is being spent somewhere else. Now that you know this, you can be more conscious of the amount you spend when you go out. You can also decide to start saving before you allow yourself to spend on other items so you can make sure you are hitting your savings goals.

Include a Reward

Have you ever noticed that when you compete in a competition or do really well in something, there's always a reward at the end? When you have to run a race at school or maybe participate in a sport, there is usually a prize for the winner. Kids that get the highest marks in class will get recognition. Even when adults go to work, there are prizes for the top performers or for reaching goals and targets. The reason this happens is that rewards are a great incentive to motivate people. This is especially true when we have to do things that we don't really want to do and that are quite difficult.

You can use this to your advantage by creating rewards at the end of doing something difficult. Creating rewards for your habits will help you stick to them because you want to get the prize at the end. A reward can be anything that motivates you. You don't have to spend a lot of money on the reward. Even something small can still be a huge motivating factor when it comes to building a habit.

Let's say one of the habits you want to get into is to start saving your money first. This is the pay-yourself-first principle that we learned earlier on in the book. If you are used to spending all your money on yourself immediately, then it might be quite difficult to start practicing this habit. Think about something you really enjoy and would be a good prize. Maybe your favorite candy bar or watching your favorite movie on Netflix. You can tell yourself that as soon as you put a specified amount of money into your savings account, you can get the prize. Even though you are doing something difficult, there is something for you to look forward to. You get to enjoy your favorite candy bar or watch your favorite movie. Your brain will start associating the hard thing with something good, and it will become a lot easier for you to do.

GETTING HELP AND SUPPORT

Even the most disciplined person needs a little bit of help when it comes to meeting their goals. I know that I've had so many good ideas, but I've never done anything to make them work. This is not because I'm not motivated or I'm lazy, but simply because there needs to be a little extra push for me to get going. You've probably experienced this every now and then. Perhaps at school, you are given an assignment or a project to do, but you end up doing it at the last minute because there are more interesting things that pop-up. I mean, somebody has to tell Netflix to stop adding new shows to the lineup!

But let's say you were doing a group project. The group needs you to pull your weight to get it done in time, so they can complete their side of the project. This is a lot more motivating because other people are relying on you, and they are holding you accountable. They will be checking up on you, and that means you will do the work a lot quicker and probably a lot better because you don't want to let someone else down or seem stupid in front of them.

It's amazing how simply being accountable to another person can unlock motivation like nothing else. I guess this is also why many schools ask parents to sign notes to confirm they have received letters or notices. Kids and teenagers would be a lot more motivated to get things done if they knew their parents were aware of them. Not only that but parents can now motivate their kids and make sure they have everything they need to get the work done.

It is pretty unlikely that you will actually reach your goals. If all you do is think about the goal in your head. In fact, you are probably going to forget about the goal and never think about it again. It's not concrete in your mind, and you haven't put it out into the world, so the chances of you reaching it is quite small. I don't mean to sound discouraging when I say this because this is not just about you but about every human. We all need something solid in order to start reaching our goals. Simply having a goal is not enough. You are only 10% likely to reach a goal when you just have the idea in your mind, and you are 95% likely to reach a goal when you have someone you are accountable to and meet with them on a regular basis (Newland, 2018). Now that's a huge leap.

This statistic shows us that we are almost 100% more likely to reach our goals when we just tell someone about it and we make sure we are accountable to them. It's such a small change, but it's going to make a huge difference. This doesn't just apply to financial goals but, basically, any other goal you have in your life. At this point, you might be wondering how to be accountable when it comes to finances. This is a great question, and it's not as difficult as you might think.

The first thing you need to do is identify somebody you can be accountable to. This person needs to be someone you trust and someone you know will give you good advice when it comes to finances. This means your best friend, who spends all his money on video games and McDonald's, is not going to be a good choice. It might be better to choose an adult or somebody older than you who is responsible for their money. They can help you think of ways you can cut down on your spending and save more. They will also be able to give you advice from what they have learned throughout their life. It doesn't have to be one of your parents. Just as long as it is somebody you trust and know is good with money.

Once you have your person in mind, you have to go to them and ask them whether they would like to be your accountability partner when it comes to handling your finances. If you explain that you have specific financial goals that you really want to reach, they will probably be happy to help you with them. Next, you'll need to set an appointment with them. These appointments are not going to be something you do once and forget about. Depending on your goals, you might need to set an appointment with them every week or every month. Just make sure they are consistent so that the person has a good idea of where you are in your financial goals. You don't have to meet face-to-face with them all the time; a phone call or video call will be good enough.

Once you have done all that, you will need to be completely transparent with your financial goals and what you hope to achieve. They will probably have some questions for you, so make sure you have the answers ready. You should know how much money you are making and exactly what your financial goals are. The other person can help you find better ways to spend your money and give you ideas on what you should be doing. Even if they don't have any groundbreaking ideas on how you can make more money or save more, just being accountable to them for your goals is so important. You can ask them to check in on you every so often so they can keep track of how well you are doing.

Simply knowing that you have to be accountable to another person is going to be life-changing. If there is a particularly difficult situation that you are going to be facing, you can let them know about it. Perhaps you know that you are going on holiday with a few of your friends and you have a weakness for overspending in this situation. You can show your accountability partner your holiday budget, and they can check in on you to make sure you are not blowing it unnecessarily.

Having somebody you are accountable to is also good for celebration and enjoying the process. You have somebody to share your wins with and to celebrate when you reach your goals. They will probably be really proud of you when you are able to get to where you want to be with your finances. Plus, it's really fun to have somebody who is walking alongside you as you reach your goals.

Quick Facts

A routine can help you create a long-lasting habit.	The 21-day habit rule is not always true. Forming a habit can take longer or shorter than that.
Writing down your habits and being specific will allow you to create habits that stick.	Rewarding yourself is the fun part of creating financial habits. Don't skip it!
Having an accountability partner can almost guarantee you reach your goals and stick to your habits.	Creating a habit is all about progress and not perfection.

CONCLUSION

Yay! We made it to the end of the book. There has truly been a lot of information you have learned and you're probably quite excited to start implementing it. As much as having all the information is a great first step, you're not going to see much change unless you actually start doing something with that information. It is so easy to learn something and forget about it. This is why the sooner you start taking action, the better it's going to be for you.

Take some time to think about what your next step is going to be. This will be different for every person because we all start from different places. If you are starting from complete scratch, I would suggest that you write out a budget first. This way, you will know how much money is coming in and what you are spending it on. From here, you can look at creating some financial goals. Start off with one or two goals, as you don't want to overwhelm yourself right from the start. Once you start getting the hang of managing your finances, you can look into other financial goals and other habits you can implement.

Another important part of finances and becoming financially successful is to continue learning. While you have already learned so much from this book, there is so much more for you to learn. The world of finances is typically always changing, and there are always new tips and tricks coming out. Especially when it comes to investing, you want to keep your finger on the pulse so you know what's going on. One of the best things you can do is subscribe to a newspaper or magazine. Many newspapers and magazines have online content that is easy to access and read. A few suggestions are The Wall Street Journal, The Economist, and Baron's. You can access a few free articles from the sources, but you will need to subscribe in order to get all the content.

Another way to get some up-to-date information is to subscribe to a podcast. Podcasts are usually free to listen to, so you can get insider information without having to pay anything. It also helps you to be productive because you can switch on a podcast and listen while you are doing something else, like cleaning your room or doing household chores. Some podcasts you can look into are *Money Girl*, *Planet Money*, and *Everyone's Talkin' Money*.

Building wealth and accessing financial freedom is a journey, so it's not going to happen with a snap of a finger. It can feel incredibly overwhelming. When you see how far you have to go and what you have to do to get there, just take it one step at a time. Think about what you have to do in the week or in the month to reach your goals. This will make things a lot more manageable, and you will feel a lot less overwhelmed. Don't worry; everyone started somewhere, and the fact that you are starting young is putting you ahead of the crowd. If you keep going along this money journey and are willing to learn and implement what you are learning, you will go far. Don't wait until it's too late to start building wealth. Start taking action toward a financially successful future with the simple steps and strategies that you found in this book!

If you found the information in this book helpful, please consider leaving a review so other people can find it. I wish you great luck and success on your financial journey! Remember, "A budget is telling your money where to go instead of wondering where it went." –Dave Ramsey

REFERENCES

Adams, R. (2023, March 13). *Goal setting strategies to help teenagers - investing money*. Young and the Invested. https://youngandtheinvested.com/goals-for-teenagers/

Affinity Credit Union. (n.d.). *5 good habits of successful investors*. Affinity Credit Union. https://www.affinitycu.ca/investing/tools-and-resources/advice/5-good-habits-of-successful-investors

Alvarez, S. (2023, March 2). *Common finance terms every newbie needs to know*. Investopedia. https://www.investopedia.com/articles/investing/061313/10-common-financial-terms-every-newbie-needs-know.asp

Annesley, J. (2015, October 27). *Top 20 inspirational quotes to develop your money mindset*. Mindset2Millions. https://www.mindset2millions.com/top-20-inspirational-quotes-money-mindset/

Atkinson, J. (2020, October 14). *The power of compound interest*. Penn Student Registration & Financial Services. https://srfs.upenn.edu/financial-wellness/blog/power-compound-interest#:~:text=When%20you%20invest%2C%20your%20account

Benson, A. (2022, November 16). *Types of real estate investments*. NerdWallet. https://www.nerdwallet.com/article/investing/types-of-real-estate-investments

BFI. (2022, September 23). *Financial risk is: Definition, types, and tips for good management*. BFI. https://www.bfi.co.id/en/blog/risiko-finansial-adalah-definisi-jenis-dan-tips-manajemen-yang-baik#:~:text=This%20is%20included%20in%20the

Bieber, C. (2022, June 16). *15 tips for recovering from a financial mistake*. The Motley Fool. https://www.fool.com/slideshow/15-tips-for-recovering-from-a-financial-mistake/

Brian Tracy's Self Improvement & Professional Development Blog. (2020, November 13). *How to develop a positive money mindset | brian tracy*. Brian Tracy's Self Improvement & Professional Development

Blog. https://www.briantracy.com/blog/financial-success/how-to-develop-a-positive-money-mindset/

BuyProperly. (2022, January 19). *Why invest in real estate: 7 key benefits to know*. BuyProperly. https://buyproperly.ca/resource-center/posts/why-invest-in-real-estate

CFA Institute. (n.d.). *Real estate investments*. CFA Institute. https://www.cfainstitute.org/en/membership/professional-development/refresher-readings/real-estate-investments

Consumer Financial Protection Bureau. (n.d.-a). *Adult financial education tools and resources*. Consumer Financial Protection Bureau. https://www.consumerfinance.gov/consumer-tools/educator-tools/adult-financial-education/tools-and-resources/

Consumer Financial Protection Bureau. (n.d.-b). *Financial habits and norms*. Consumer Financial Protection Bureau. https://www.consumerfinance.gov/consumer-tools/educator-tools/youth-financial-education/learn/financial-habits-norms/

Copper. (n.d.). *Ultimate guide: Copper's guide to budgeting (for teens)*. Copper. https://www.getcopper.com/guide/budgeting

Credit Counselling Society. (n.d.-a). *How to identify income & expenses for your budget*. Credit Counselling Society. https://nomoredebts.org/budgeting/build-household-budget/separate-income-from-expenses-step-2

Credit Counselling Society. (n.d.-b). *Money management tips for teens*. Credit Counselling Society. https://nomoredebts.org/budgeting/budgeting-for-teens

Debt.org. (n.d.). *Credit explained: What is it and why is it important?* Debt.org. https://www.debt.org/credit/#:~:text=The%20main%20difference%20between%20credit

DePaul, K. (2021, February 2). *What does it really take to build a new habit?* Harvard Business Review. https://hbr.org/2021/02/what-does-it-really-take-to-build-a-new-habit

Doghudje, K. (2016, January 24). *20 inspirational money quotes to set you on the path to wealth*. Businessday NG. https://businessday.ng/uncategorized/article/20-inspirational-money-quotes-to-set-you-on-the-path-to-wealth/#:~:text=Money%20is%20meant%20to%20serve

Elkaslassy, L. (2018, April 25). *How to understand and overcome your limiting beliefs around money.* Laura Elkaslassy & Co. Coaching. https://www.lauraelkaslassy.com/limiting-money-beliefs/

EU Business School. (2022, August 16). *How to identify business opportunities in any market.* EU Business School. https://www.euruni.edu/blog/how-to-identify-business-opportunities-in-any-market/

Financial Samurai. (2021, January 3). *What percent of americans own stocks?* Financial Samurai. https://www.financialsamurai.com/what-percent-of-americans-own-stocks/#:~:text=As%20of%202021%2C%20the%20top

Garrate, C. (2022, June 25). *The impact of artificial intelligence on kids and teens.* Aimagazine.com. https://aimagazine.com/machine-learning/the-impact-of-artificial-intelligence-on-kids-and-teens

Gillespie, P. (2015, April 28). *Meet the 17-year-old investor who tripled his money.* CNNMoney. https://money.cnn.com/2015/04/28/investing/millennial-investor-17-year-old-brandon-fleisher/

Go Henry. (2022, October 10). *Common financial problems for teens and how to resolve them.* Go Henry. https://www.gohenry.com/uk/blog/financial-education/common-financial-problems-for-teens-and-how-to-resolve-them

Gobler, E. (2022, June 20). *Investing guide for teens (and parents).* The Balance. https://www.thebalancemoney.com/investing-guide-for-teens-and-parents-4588018#:~:text=Some%20of%20the%20best%20investments

Gordon-Barnes, C. (2014, October 12). *6 fresh ways to find your passion.* The Muse; The Muse. https://www.themuse.com/advice/6-fresh-ways-to-find-your-passion

Grossman, A. (2021, December 27). *11 common (and surprising) teenage financial problems.* Money Prodigy. https://www.moneyprodigy.com/teenage-financial-problems/

Hakeenah, N. (2022, March 9). *Why personal accountability is the key to financial success.* Money254. https://www.money254.co.ke/post/

why-personal-accountability-is-the-key-to-financial-success-money-management

Harbour, S. (2021, October 22). *4 savings accounts for investors*. Investopedia. https://www.investopedia.com/articles/personal-finance/090314/4-savings-accounts-investors.asp

Hathaway, J. (2022, November 13). *Everything you need to know about cultivating a "wealth mindset."* Real Simple. https://www.realsimple.com/work-life/money/wealth-mindset

Huang, E. (n.d.). *10 money management tips for teens*. Echo Wealth Management. https://www.echowealthmanagement.com/blog/10-money-management-tips-teens

Indeed. (2022, November 22). *14 characteristics of an entrepreneur*. Indeed. https://ca.indeed.com/career-advice/career-development/entrepreneur-characteristics?aceid=&gclid=Cj0KCQjw3a2iBhCFARIsAD4jQB3YS_vMZjR4JuuxyABIJR-5su_-WTAdWk18LSdzcjbsEXHERnktEdAaAlUGEALw_wcB&gclsrc=aw.ds

Insurance Information Institute. (n.d.). *How to build and maintain a good credit history*. Insurance Information Institute. https://www.iii.org/article/how-can-i-build-and-maintain-good-credit-history#:~:text=Your%20proven%20ability%20to%20manage

Investopedia. (n.d.). *Credit & debt: Managing both wisely*. Investopedia. https://www.investopedia.com/credit-and-debt-4689724

Irby, L. (2022, March 31). *7 best ways to build good credit*. The Balance. https://www.thebalancemoney.com/ways-to-build-good-credit-960109

Island Savings. (n.d.). *11 ways to stick to your budget*. Island Savings. https://www.islandsavings.ca/simple-advice/money/ways-to-stick-to-your-budget

Kagan, J. (2019). *Compound interest definition*. Investopedia. https://www.investopedia.com/terms/c/compoundinterest.asp

Karr, A. (2023, May 3). *Why it's important to save money at an early age*. Mydoh. https://www.mydoh.ca/learn/money-101/why-kids-and-teens-should-start-saving-money-early/

Knueven, L. (2022, December 9). *How to save money as a teenager so you can get yourself a car, pay for college, or take a trip*. Business Insider.

https://www.businessinsider.com/personal-finance/how-to-save-money-as-a-teenager

Kurt, D. (2023, March 23). *Best resources for improving financial literacy.* Investopedia. https://www.investopedia.com/best-resources-for-improving-financial-literacy-5091689

Lake, R. (2022, March 16). *6 types of savings accounts.* Forbes Advisor. https://www.forbes.com/advisor/banking/savings/types-of-savings-accounts/

Marquit, M. (2023, March 3). *Financial goals for students: How and why to set them.* Investopedia. https://www.investopedia.com/financial-goals-for-students-7151682#:~:text=Financial%20Goals%20Early%3F-

MBDA. (2010, July 20). *8 traits of successful entrepreneurs--Do you have what it takes?* Minority Business Development Agency. https://archive.mbda.gov/news/blog/2010/07/8-traits-successful-entrepreneurs-do-you-have-what-it-takes.html

Milliken, M. (2022, August 26). *12 easy ways to cut expenses at home.* Debt.org. https://www.debt.org/advice/how-to-cut-expenses/

Mint. (2020, August 25). *6 Ways to Instill a Positive Money Mindset.* Mint-Life Blog. https://mint.intuit.com/blog/personal-finance/6-ways-to-instill-a-positive-money-mindset/

Mint. (2022, January 18). *23 better money habits you need to start doing in 2022.* MintLife Blog. https://mint.intuit.com/blog/planning/better-money-habits/

Money for the Mamas. (2021, January 10). *50+ budgeting quotes to motivate you (and your bottom line).* Money for the Mamas. https://www.moneyforthemamas.com/budgeting-quotes/#:~:text=%E2%80%9CA%20budget%20tells%20us%20what

Money Mentors. (n.d.-a). *How chris paid off $47,000 of consumer debt.* Money Mentors. https://moneymentors.ca/resources/stories/how-chris-paid-off-47000-of-consumer-debt/

Money Mentors. (n.d.-b). *How to move forward after a financial mistake.* Money Mentors. https://moneymentors.ca/money-tips/how-to-love-yourself-after-a-financial-mistake/

Morris, G. (2021, November 18). *12 ways to cut your expenses & save money*. InCharge Debt Solutions. https://www.incharge.org/finan cial-literacy/budgeting-saving/how-to-cut-your-expenses/

Muller, C. (2022, September 5). *Best investments for teens - 9 ways to get your teens to invest*. Dough Roller. https://www.doughroller.net/investing/best-investments-for-teens/

Newland, S. (2018). *The power of accountability*. AFCPE. https://www.afcpe.org/news-and-publications/the-standard/2018-3/the-power-of-accountability/

Nolo. (n.d.). *Avoiding financial trouble: Ten tips*. Nolo. https://www.nolo.com/legal-encyclopedia/avoiding-financial-trouble-ten-tips-29485.html

Norada Real Estate Investments. (2021, September 7). *10 tips to be successful in real estate investing*. Norada Real Estate Investments. https://www.noradarealestate.com/blog/10-ways-successful-real-estate-investment/

O'neill, B. (2009, February). *The benefits of saving money (rutgers NJAES)*. Njaes.rutgers.edu. https://njaes.rutgers.edu/sshw/message/message.php?p=Finance&m=122#:~:text=Saving%20provides%20a%20financial%20E2%80%9Cbackstop

O'Shea, A. (2021, March 12). *How to invest in real estate: 5 ways to get started*. NerdWallet. https://www.nerdwallet.com/article/investing/5-ways-to-invest-in-real-estate

O'Shea, B., & Schwahn, L. (2021, January 13). *Budgeting 101: How to budget money*. NerdWallet. https://www.nerdwallet.com/article/finance/how-to-budget

Oak, R. (2022, August 3). *Top 7 reasons why 90% of US millionaires invest in real estate & why you should follow the lead*. Red Oak Development Group. https://redoakvc.com/top-7-reasons-why-90-of-us-millionaires-invest-in-real-estate-why-you-should-follow-the-lead/#:~:text=%E2%80%9C90%25%20of%20all%20millionaires%20become

Paris, D. (2023, May 3). *8 reasons why financial literacy is important*. Mydoh. https://www.mydoh.ca/learn/money-101/8-reasons-to-teach-financial-literacy-to-kids-teens/#:~:text=By%20teaching%20kids%20about%20money

Practical Money Skills. (n.d.). *Evaluating your finances*. Practical Money

Skills. https://www.practicalmoneyskills.com/learn/budgeting/evaluating_your_finances

Ramsey Solutions. (n.d.). *How to stick to your budget.* Ramsey Solutions. https://www.ramseysolutions.com/budgeting/steps-to-help-you-stick-to-your-budget

RBC Wealth Management. (n.d.). *Why financial literacy is an important life skill for youths.* RBC Wealth Management. https://www.rbcwealthmanagement.com/en-ca/insights/why-financial-literacy-is-an-important-life-skill-for-youths

Ronis, H. (2023, January 31). *How to start a business as a teenager.* WikiHow. https://www.wikihow.com/Start-a-Business-As-a-Teenager

Rose, S. (2022, November 28). *Financial literacy quotes.* OppLoans. https://www.opploans.com/oppu/articles/quotes-financial-literacy/#:~:text=%E2%80%9CFinancial%20literacy%20is%20the%20ability

Royale, O. (2020, October 20). *14 teen entrepreneurs and how they succeeded.* Oxford Royale Academy. https://www.oxford-royale.com/articles/14-teen-entrepreneurs/

Rule 1 Investing. (n.d.). *Types of investments.* Rule 1 Investing. https://www.ruleoneinvesting.com/investing-guide/types-of-investments/?network=g&utm1=&gc_id=19978600309&h_ad_id=654987284305&utm_source=google&utm_medium=cpc&utm_campaign=&utm_content=&utm_term=&hsa_acc=8939821212&hsa_cam=19978600309&hsa_grp=148438539015&hsa_ad=654987284305&hsa_src=g&hsa_tgt=aud-1961450892464:dsa-1122117810636&hsa_kw=&hsa_mt=&hsa_net=adwords&hsa_ver=3&gad=1&gclid=Cj0KCQjw3a2iBhCFARIsAD4jQB1zNDGQIcIqYFGJPLAJAMv8fVxcS5QX8BcumtMhlMLxT7zyvQK5sEIaAoq3EALw_wcB

Shopify. (2022, August 4). *What is entrepreneurship? Definition and guide for 2022.* Shopify. https://www.shopify.com/ca/blog/what-is-entrepreneurship

Shubel, M. (2022, September 1). *How to overcome your limiting beliefs about money.* Clever Girl Finance. https://www.clevergirlfinance.com/building-wealth/financial-empowerment/money-mindset/

limiting-beliefs-about-money/

Stanford Online. (n.d.). *What is entrepreneurship?* Stanford Online. https://online.stanford.edu/what-is-entrepreneurship

Stowers, J. (2019). *A step by step guide to starting a business.* Business News Daily. https://www.businessnewsdaily.com/4686-how-to-start-a-business.html

StudySmarter UK. (n.d.). *Basic financial terms: Definitions & statements.* StudySmarter UK. https://www.studysmarter.co.uk/explanations/business-studies/introduction-to-business/basic-financial-terms/#:~:text=Revenue%2C%20costs%2C%20profit%20and%20loss

The Investopedia Team. (2020). *A real estate investing guide.* Investopedia. https://www.investopedia.com/mortgage/real-estate-investing-guide/

The Jed Foundation. (n.d.). *How to deal with financial stress.* The Jed Foundation. https://jedfoundation.org/resource/how-to-deal-with-financial-stress/

ThinkImpact. (2022, July 20). *47+ entrepreneur statistics (full list 2023) ++ charts.* ThinkImpact. https://www.thinkimpact.com/entrepreneur-statistics/#:~:text=Within%20their%20first%2010%20years

Velocity Club. (2023, February). *The importance of your mindset in building wealth.* Velocity Club. https://www.velocityclub.co.za/blog/2023/2/the-importance-of-your-mindset-in-building-wealth

WallStreetMojo. (2022, April 1). *Real estate investing.* WallStreetMojo. https://www.wallstreetmojo.com/real-estate-investing/

White, J. (2023, February 2). *The majority of teens feel unprepared to finance their future.* Savingforcollege. https://www.savingforcollege.com/article/majority-of-teens-feel-unprepared-to-finance-their-future#:~:text=February%202%2C%202023-

Wong, R. (2021, January 14). *9 inspiring financial stories.* YNAB. https://www.ynab.com/9-inspiring-financial-stories/

IMAGE REFERENCES

Barbhuiya, T. (2021, October 21). A man holding a jar with a savings label on it [Image]. Unsplash. https://unsplash.com/photos/0ITvgXAU5Oo

ErikaWittlieb. (2017, July 8). Summer lemonade stand [Image]. Pexels. https://pixabay.com/photos/lemonade-stand-lemonade-summer-2483297/

Evans, A. (2020, May 18). A person holding credit cards against a white background wall [Image]. Unsplashed. https://unsplash.com/photos/RJQE64NmC_o

Grabowska, K. (2020, May 7). Crop anonymous financier planning budget writing numbers in notebook [Image]. Pexels. https://www.pexels.com/photo/crop-anonymous-financier-planning-budget-writing-numbers-in-notebook-4386339/

Li, K. (2021, October 20). Symbolic house made from one hundred dollars isolated on white background [Image]. Unsplashed. https://unsplash.com/photos/1sCXwVoqKAw

Nekrashevich, A. (2021, February 4). Businessman with stock market on laptop [Iimage]. Pexels. https://www.pexels.com/photo/marketing-businessman-person-hands-6801647/

Wilcox, K. (2017, September 16). Four Men Sitting on Platform [Image]. Pexels. https://www.pexels.com/photo/four-men-sitting-on-platform-923657/

www.ingramcontent.com/pod-product-compliance
Lightning Source LLC
Chambersburg PA
CBHW070318010526
44107CB00004B/350